A Mind Spread Out
on the Ground

A MIND SPREAD OUT
ON THE GROUND

ALICIA ELLIOTT

THORNDIKE PRESS
A part of Gale, a Cengage Company

**LIBRARY OF CONGRESS CIP DATA ON FILE.
CATALOGUING IN PUBLICATION FOR THIS BOOK
IS AVAILABLE FROM THE LIBRARY OF CONGRESS.**

ISBN-13: 978-1-4328-8539-7 (hardcover alk. paper)

Published in 2021 by arrangement with Melville House Publishing

Printed in Mexico
Print Number: 01   Print Year: 2021

*For the people who always
made me feel like I mattered:
Mom, Dad, Mike*

CONTENTS

CONTENTS

7

A MIND SPREAD OUT
ON THE GROUND

He took his glasses off and rubbed the bridge of his nose the way men in movies do whenever they encounter a particularly vexing woman.

"I'm really confused. You need to give me something here.

What's making you depressed?"

His reaction made me think briefly of residential schools — the state-mandated, church-run boarding schools Indigenous kids were sent to "kill the Indian, and save the man." At the time I couldn't understand the connection between the two. Maybe it was the fact that he operated his therapy sessions out of a church. That certainly didn't help.

I wasn't sure what to say. Can a metaphor or simile capture depression? It was definitely heavy, but could I really compare it to a weight? Weight in and of itself is not devastating; depression is. At times it made me short of breath and at times it had the potential to be deadly, but was it really like drowning? At least with drowning others could see the flailing limbs and splashing water and know you needed help. Depression could slip in entirely unnoticed and dress itself up as normalcy, so when it finally took hold others would be so surprised they wouldn't know how to pull you to safety. They'd stand there staring — good-intentioned but helpless. Empathetic, perhaps, but mute. Or, as in the case of this particularly unqualified therapist, angry and accusing. Not that I necessarily blame them. I've done the same thing.

When what was left of my family moved to the Six Nations of the Grand River reserve in Ontario, Canada, we lived in a two-bedroom trailer — my sister and I in the smaller room, my three younger brothers in the master bedroom. My parents had no bedroom, no bed. They slept in the living room on the couch and recliner. As one may assume of such circumstances, privacy was precious, if it existed at all. Doors never stayed closed for long; at any moment someone could barrel in unannounced. This meant there was no place for my mother to hide her illness.

I'd mostly known her as having bipolar disorder, though she'd been diagnosed and rediagnosed many times. Postpartum depression, manic depression, schizophrenia. Most recently, my mother has been diagnosed as having either schizoaffective disorder, which is a version of bipolar disorder with elements of schizophrenia, or posttraumatic stress disorder, depending on which doctor you talk to. None of these phrases gave her relief. In fact, they often seemed to hurt her, turning every feeling she had into yet another symptom of yet another disease.

What these words meant to my siblings and me was that our mother's health was on a timer. We didn't know when the timer would go off, but when it did, our happy, playful, hilarious mother would disappear behind a curtain and another would emerge: alternatively angry and mournful, wired and lethargic. When she was depressed she'd become almost entirely silent. She'd lie on our brother's bottom bunk and blink at us, her soft limp limbs spilling onto the stained, slate-coloured carpet. I'd sit on the floor beside her, smooth her hair — bottle red with grey moving in like a slow tide — and ask her what was wrong. She'd stay silent but her face would transform. Damp, swol-

11

len, violet, as if the words she couldn't say were bubbling beneath her skin, burning her up from the inside.

Terminology is tricky. Initially, depression was known as "melancholia," a word that first brought to my mind a field of blue cornflower and golden hay. Its trochaic metre gave it an inherent poeticism, an ingrained elegance. It was delicate, feminine. Hamlet's doomed lover, Ophelia, definitely did not suffer from depression. When she floated down that river, decked in garlands, stones in her pockets, she was in the throes of *melancholia.*

The term first appeared in Mesopotamian texts in the second century BCE. At the time, they considered melancholia a form of demonic possession. They weren't alone: ancient Babylonian, Chinese and Egyptian civilizations all attributed mental illness to demons overpowering the spiritually weak. Exorcism — which often entailed beatings, restraint and starvation — was the only known "cure." Even during the Renaissance, when thinking about depression began to reflect the more progressive views of the early Greek physician Hippocrates, a heavily Christian Europe had another way to describe those with mental illness: witches. They were "cured" by being burned at the stake. Sometimes, as part of their trial, suspected witches underwent an ordeal by water. They were tied to a rope and thrown from a boat. If they sank they'd be pulled back to a safety of sorts, their innocence proven, but their illness unchecked. If they floated, like Ophelia, they were considered a witch and summarily executed.

My quite Catholic mother believes demonic possession is a real danger. She pretty much used the 1973 film *The Exorcist* as an instructional video for my siblings and me. It was mostly effective. I played with a Ouija board only once, reluctantly, and though I remained firmly in control of my body, I still try to avoid the game (and pictures of Linda Blair) at all costs. I know demonic possession is impossible, probably, but it still scares me more than I'd like to admit.

So when my mother, now living in an adult care home in Florida, told me she was hearing demonic voices and thought she needed an exorcism, I was legitimately terrified. Not because I thought she was possessed — she didn't mention anything about floating above her bed, and her voice sounded normal. I was scared for her. She truly believed demons were real and could take control of the spiritually weak. If she believed she was being overtaken by these demons, logic dictated that *she* was spiritually weak. As if her depressed mind didn't have enough to guilt her with.

She wouldn't tell me what the voices were saying to her. She just reiterated over and over that she was a sinner, that she had impure thoughts, that she hadn't been going to church enough. None of this seemed to me like enough reason to call in an exorcist.

Evidently her priest down in Florida disagreed. He said it did, indeed, sound like she was in the midst of a spiritual battle, that she should contact the church about sending an exorcist right away. Though he himself was part of the Catholic Church, he never offered any assistance with her "spiritual battle," never offered to bring in an exorcist to slay her inner demon. He just gave her his half-baked opinion like a torch and watched as she caught flame.

As far as analogies go, comparing depression to a demon is a pretty good one. Both overtake your faculties, leaving you disconnected and disembodied. Both change you so abruptly that even your loved ones barely recognize you. Both whisper evil words and malformed truths. Both scare most people shitless.

■ ■ ■

According to Diane Purkiss's *The Witch in History: Early Modern and Twentieth-Century Representations,* European colonists widely considered Indigenous peoples to be devil worshippers. In fact, during the Salem witch trials, the people of the Sagamore tribe were blamed — described by early Puritan minister and mastermind of the witch trials, Cotton Mather, as "horrid sorcerers, and hellish conjurors . . . [who] conversed with Demons." One person on trial claimed to have attended a black mass with the Sagamore Indians. Mercy Short, another accused witch, took it one step further: she claimed the Devil himself was an Indian, describing him as "not of a Negro, but of a tawny, or an Indian color."

Literal demonizing of Indigenous people was a natural extension of early tactics used to move colonization along. In 1452 and 1455 the Catholic Church issued papal bulls calling for non-Christian people to be invaded, robbed and enslaved under the premise that they were "enemies of Christ." Forty years later, when Christopher Columbus accidentally arrived in the Americas, European monarchs began to expand on the ideas contained in those bulls, issuing policies and practices that have been collectively referred to as the Doctrine of Discovery. These new policies dictated that "devil-worshipping" Indigenous peoples worldwide should not even be thought of as humans, and thus the land they had cared for and inhabited for centuries was *terra nullius,* or vacant land, and Christian monarchs had the "right" to claim it all. The Doctrine of Discovery was such a tantalizing, seemingly guilt-free justification for genocide, even U.S. Secretary of State Thomas Jefferson adopted it as official policy in 1792 — and we all know how much Americans wanted to distinguish themselves from Europe at the time.

The Doctrine of Discovery is still cited in court cases today whenever Canada or the U.S. want to shut up Indigenous tribes who complain. In an attempt to stop this lazy, racist rationale, a delegation of Indigenous people went to Rome in 2016 to ask the church to rescind these papal bulls. Kahnawake Mohawk Kenneth Deer said that after hearing their concerns, Pope Francis merely looked him in the eye and said, "I'll pray for you." Two years later, after the delegation's second trip to Rome to discuss these papal bulls, they were told the matter was being sent to another committee. Nothing else has been done, though presumably the Pope is still praying for us.

"Can you imagine going to a funeral every day, maybe even two funerals, for five to ten years?" the Haudenosaunee chief asks. He's giving a decolonization presentation, talking about the way colonization has affected our people since contact. Smallpox, tuberculosis, even the common cold hit our communities particularly hard. Then, on top of that, we had wars to contend with — some against the French, some against the British, some against either or neither or both. Back then death was all you could see, smell, hear or taste. Death was all you could feel.

"What does that type of mourning, pain and loss do to you?" he asks. We reflect on our own losses, our own mourning, our own pain. We say nothing.

After a moment he answers himself. "It creates numbness."

Numbness is often how people describe their experience of depression.

I was sixteen when I wrote my first suicide note. I was alone in my room, for once. It was cold; the fire in our wood-burning stove must have gone out. I was huddled beneath the unzipped sleeping bag I used as a comforter, listening to the only modern rock station my ancient radio could pick up. The songs washed over me. My brothers laughing, crashing and crying washed over me. My mother half-heartedly yelling at them while she watched a movie with my sister washed over me. My father's absence washed over me.

Even though the trailer was full I was alone. I was alone and I felt nothing and it hurt so much. More than grief, more than anger. I just wanted it to end.

Tears fell on the paper faster than I could write. It was hard to read in parts. I didn't care. As long as it reassured my family they shouldn't blame themselves, it would do the trick.

I looked at the knife I'd smuggled from the kitchen, pressed its edge to my wrist. Nothing happened. The blade was too dull.

I'd have to stab hard and slash deep just to break the skin. I was crying so hard.

I reread my note. I looked back at the knife. Even though it could hardly peel a potato it scared me more than the void I felt.

I lay back down, disgusted with myself and

my lack of resolve. I tried to listen to the radio. I couldn't hear anything.

Though suicide was quite rare for Onkwehon:we pre-contact, after contact and the subsequent effects of colonialism it has ballooned so much that, as of 2013, suicide and self-inflicted injuries are the leading cause of death for Native people living in Canada under the age of forty-four. A 2019 study revealed that, since 1999, the suicide rate among Native men living in the U.S. has gone up 71 per cent. The suicide rate for Native women is an even more staggering 139 per cent. Native youth in America face a suicide rate two and a half times the national average, with suicide being the second leading cause of death for Native youth between the ages of ten and twenty-four. For LGBTQ2S+ Onkwehon:we, no data exists.

Interestingly, the Centre for Suicide Prevention has found lower rates of depression and suicide among communities that exhibit "cultural continuity." This includes self-government, land control, control over education and cultural activities, and command of police, fire and health services. In other words, the less Canada maintains its historical role as the abusive father, micro-managing and undermining First Nations at every turn, the better off the people are.

Lower instances of suicide were also found in communities where more than 50 percent of the people spoke their Indigenous language. This probably isn't much of a surprise to an Indigenous person. We know our cultures have meaning and worth, that that culture lives and breathes inside our languages.

The U.S. and Canada knew that, too. Which is why they fought so hard to make us forget them.

There are two scientific designations for depression. The droller, more scientific term for melancholia is "endogenous depression." In contrast to exogenous, or reactive, depression — which stems from a major event such as divorce, job loss or death in the family — melancholic depression has no apparent outside cause. In other words, it comes out of the blue. This is a rather ridiculous way of putting it when you consider that depression itself is sometimes referred to as "the blues." The blues coming out of the blue. Go figure.

I've heard one person translate a Mohawk phrase for depression to, roughly, "his mind fell to the ground." I ask my sister about this. She's been studying Mohawk for the past three years and is practically fluent. She's raising her daughter to be the same. They're the first members of our family to speak the language since our paternal grandfather a handful of decades ago.

"Wake'nikonhra'kwenhtará:'on," she says. "It's not quite 'fell to the ground.' It's more like, 'His mind is . . .' " She pauses. She repeats the word in Mohawk. Slows it down. Considers what English words in her arsenal can best approximate the phrase. " 'His mind is . . .' " She moves her hands around, palms down, as if doing a large, messy finger painting. "Literally stretched or sprawled out on the ground. It's all over." She explains there's another phrase, too. Wake'nikonhrèn:ton. It means "the mind is suspended."

Both words indicate an inability to concentrate. That's one of the signs of depression. I know because I've checked it off in the copy of *Mind Over Mood* I took out from the library. It says my depression currently scores a 32 out of a possible 57, or 56 percent. Not the worst. At least I'm not considering suicide. Suicidal thoughts is number ten on the checklist.

There is nothing in the book about the importance of culture, nothing about intergenerational trauma, racism, sexism, colonialism, homophobia, transphobia. As if depression doesn't "see" petty things like race or gender or sexual orientation.

"We're all just people, man," melancholia mutters, pushing its white-boy dreads aside as it passes me a joint.

I've heard people say that when you learn a people's language, you learn their culture. It tells you how they think of the world, how they experience it. That's why translation is so difficult — you have to take one way of seeing the world and translate it to another, while still piecing the words together so they make sense.

Lately I've been thinking a lot about why there is no Mohawk word to differentiate between reactive and melancholic depression. No scientific jargon to legitimize and pathologize. Just wake'nikonhrèn:ton and wake'nikonhra'kwenhtará:'on. A mind hanging by a thread, and a mind spread out on the ground. A before and an after — the same way we measure ourselves against colonialism. What does that mean about our culture?

If we had had more terms and definitions backing up our understanding of depression, would we have been better equipped to deal with it when its effects began tearing our communities apart? Would those who wanted to civilize us have been more open to listening to our pain if we'd used their words? How much could "endogenous," "exogenous," "depression" or "melancholia" have helped when they're all essentially referring to the same thing? How many ways do we need to describe a person in pain that needs help to heal?

Is there a language of depression? I'm not sure. Depression often seems to me like the exact opposite of language. It takes your tongue, your thoughts, your self-worth, and leaves an empty vessel. Not that different from colonialism, actually. In fact, the *Mind Over Mood* Depression Inventory could double as a checklist for the effects of colonialism on our people. Sad or depressed mood? Check. Feelings of guilt? Check. Irritability? Considering how fast my dad's side of the family are to yell, check. Finding it harder than usual to do things? Well, Canada tried to eradicate our entire way of being, then forced us to take on their values and wondered why we couldn't cope. Definite check. Low self-esteem, self-critical thoughts, tiredness or loss of energy, difficulty making decisions, seeing the future as hopeless, recurrent thoughts of death, suicidal thoughts? Check, check, check.

And if colonialism is like depression, and the Onkwehon:we suffering from it are witches, then I guess it shouldn't surprise anyone that our treatment has always been the same: to light us on fire and let us burn.

I now understand why that therapist in that church reminded me of residential schools. When I think of that man sitting across from me, chastising me for not saying the right words, the words that made it easy for him to understand me and cure me, I think of how my great-grandparents felt when priests and nuns did the same to them. The difference is that the therapist was trying to cure me of being depressed; those priests and nuns were trying to cure my ancestors of being Indian. In some ways they succeeded. In many they did not.

Both depression and colonialism have stolen my language in different ways. I know this. I feel it inside me even as I struggle to explain it. But that does not mean I have to accept it. I struggle against colonialism the same way I struggle against depression — by telling myself that I'm not worthless, that I'm not a failure, that things will get better. That every breath I choose to take is a tiny revolution, a rebellion against the forces that tell me I should stop.

My people are the Mohawk, one of six nations that make up the Haudenosaunee Confederacy. Our Confederacy Chiefs Council inspired the structure of American democracy. Our Great Law inspired the American Constitution. We are people with a rich history, with complex, nuanced understandings of leadership, diplomacy and responsibility. A mind suspended in the air. A mind spread out on the ground. In a way, these translations show exactly who we are. We are poets: crafting precise, beautiful comparisons to the world we know in order to make the abstract understood. We are linguistic caretakers: piecing together the most precise descriptions of your ailments that we can, wanting to acknowledge what has happened to you without blaming you, working to make sure you feel understood.

The Haudenosaunee condolence ceremony shows the same level of care, poeticism and insight. It was originally created by Hiawatha, an Onondaga leader who helped bring five warring nations together in peace to form the Haudenosaunee Confederacy. Hiawatha created the condolence ceremony to help a person in mourning after a death. Whoever is conducting the condolence recites the Requickening Ad-

25

dress as they offer the grieving person three strands of wampum, one at a time.

One: soft, white deer cloth is used to wipe the tears from their eyes so they can see the beauty of creation again.

Two: a soft feather is used to remove the dust from their ears so they can hear the kind words of those around them.

Three: water, the original medicine, is used to wash away the dust settled in their throats that keeps them from speaking, from breathing, from reconnecting with the world outside their grief.

I know this is supposed to be a ceremony for people with reactive depression caused by a death. As far as I know there is no condolence ceremony for those Onkwehon:we suffering from melancholia — those who are, in effect, mourning themselves. There's no collective condolence ceremony for our people, either — those who need help to see our beauty and hear our songs and speak our language. But maybe, one day, there can be.

Things that were stolen once can be stolen back.

Half-Breed
A Racial Biography
in Five Parts

1 Dental hygiene was a self-directed exercise in my childhood home, which meant it didn't happen. Unused toothbrushes sat stiff-bristled and impeccable in cups beside the sink. I only ever noticed a smell on my father's breath, though: an alcoholic bitterness. The smell usually corresponded with the subwoofer trembling at midnight, spitting out Bonnie Raitt and other smooth-voiced saints of heartbreak.

I separated my father into two entities: the one who played *Resident Evil* with us for hours, laughing when a zombie jumped out and scared him, then sneaking outside to bang on the living room window to scare us in turn, and the one who stared at me dead-eyed when I asked him to turn down his drunken music. Mom never bothered to explain why Dad's voice was so loud and slurred. I had no clue my father was having problems weaving himself into the tapestry of white suburban bliss. I never knew about the promotions he'd seen slip past him despite being one of the top salesmen in every company he worked for. I never knew about the rampant alcoholism on his side of the family, its body count. All I knew was when we went down to Six Nations for the powwow, all my aunts and uncles and cousins were loud and laughing, too, their breath the same scent I then considered genetic. They didn't dote on my siblings and me the same way they doted on my cousins, pinching their cheeks with one hand, holding a beer bottle in the other. But at least there was musical consistency: Bonnie Raitt always there, crooning me awake.

2 In second grade I went to Native American Magnet School #19 in Buffalo, New York. Part of its mandate was to provide a class for its handful of Native kids to learn Native culture. Every day we would slip away from the droning arithmetic of our classrooms into a space dispassionately hung with dreamcatchers and laminated warriors. The curriculum was a grab bag of general knowledge. What the Navajo ate, what the Oneida wore. Neat, bloodless trivia isolated from historical context. They'd show us teepees and longhouses and adobes

drawn over state lines, as if we could belong in America as easily as those sketches on that map. Then we'd sneak back to our regular classes and continue like we never left, a collective amnesia settling over us.

There was one white girl in my Native class: Regina. She wanted to make crafts and sing songs with her best friend, Brittany, so her parents claimed a sliver of Cherokee ancestry and the school let her in. I hated this, because I hated Regina. Before she came along, Brittany was my best friend. The way Regina's parents successfully lied her way into *my* Native class filled me with a rage so intense it could only ever be understood by fellow vengeful seven-year-olds.

The other kids knew why we were being whisked away between math and spelling. Yet when my new best friend, a Puerto Rican girl named Rosita, saw my father and asked if he was Native, disgust curdling her words, I paused. She couldn't already tell? Where did she think I went every day?

I had never really considered it before, but I looked more like Regina than I did my father. It was as if his genes had skipped over me entirely. I realized then I had a choice. I'd fallen down a rabbit hole into a racial Wonderland where logic was negotiable. Only I wasn't Alice; I was the Cheshire Cat, the Trickster. If I wanted I could say I was part Mexican or Italian or Mongolian, and the person would squint, but nod. As though they accepted that America's melting pot would sooner or later boil all races down to a pale person like me.

"He's not Native. He's Puerto Rican."

Like Regina, I could pretend.

I waited to be called out as a fraud, for my father to stride over and tell everyone the truth. But nothing happened. Incredibly, Rosita believed me. I was too cool to be Native anyway, she rationalized, too clean. She cemented our newfound racial sisterhood with a necklace of the Puerto Rican flag cleverly assembled from red, white and blue pony beads.

I wore that necklace with an absurd, anxious pride, wondering whether Regina felt the same uneasiness when she brought home her construction paper headdresses and three sisters soup recipes.

3 My mother, like any good Catholic, raised us in the faith. We were fed divine mercy chaplets and patron saints more often than food. Even my steely-willed father wasn't immune; he converted to Catholicism for her eventually. I still remember his baptism.

It was a bizarre tableau, a scene from some forgotten fairy tale: a giant Native man hunched over a stone fountain meant for babies as water spilled from his thick black hair. After that he dutifully sat in the pews with us on Sundays, silent and focused until he had to shut us up with a furrowed glare.

When I was thirteen we moved to Six Nations. Dad started going to Longhouse and getting involved in sticky rez politics. Staying out long and sleeping deep. Finding his roots, he said. Mom said roots were nothing if they led to Hell. All her prayers' intentions were for his recommitment to Catholicism. While we kids droned half-heartedly through every Hail Mary, her prayers took on the tenor of threats. She claimed she was just worried about Dad's soul, but it was more than that. Every step he took towards his Native identity was another step away from her. With us she felt the same. If we ever went to Longhouse she'd rant for hours about how we weren't just Native, you know. We had other heritage and we shouldn't hide it. Were we ashamed of our own mother?

It was around this time I started taking Canadian History in high school. We covered residential schools in broad strokes and clinical tones, giving the impression these schools were from an era long past. Kids pulled screaming out of their homes, forced to speak English and say the rosary and endure all manner of abuse, returning to families with whom they could no longer communicate. My teacher never mentioned that the Mohawk Institute, Brantford's residential school and unhappy home for over two hundred Six Nations kids, remained fully operational until 1970. I'm not entirely sure she knew, despite its having been turned into a museum a short drive away.

I asked my father if he knew the residential school was open until the '70s. "The Mush Hole? Yeah." His voice was terse, pained, as if I was picking at a scab that had just started to heal. I dropped the subject.

My curiosity was hardly sated, though. As soon as my dad went out, I explained what residential schools were to my mother. She being our family's religious ambassador, I asked her how members of the Catholic Church could do such awful things to children. She hesitated. Then, with a politician's duplicitous finesse, she said that while those priests and nuns were extreme, they did save many Indian kids' souls. They probably thought they were doing God's will. It seemed strange that she — the most compassionate person I'd ever met — was defending such abusive methods of indoctrination, as if Heaven were a gang you got jumped into. "It was another time," she said. "They had different ideas then."

She'd start a rosary just as my father was supposed to get home from some community meeting. A door slam would announce his entrance and just as quickly his exit. My mother's face was like shards of glass, broken but dangerous.

4 On the hour-long bus ride from our homes in Six Nations to our high school in Brantford, Ontario, one person was wordlessly, unanimously agreed upon as the bus punching bag. Most years it was Ryan. His sloped forehead, large stature and passive nature proved an irresistible cocktail to the violent and otherwise insecure. That is, until Ryan's mother pulled him off the bus and Carrie came along. I was in eleventh grade, she was in ninth grade: loud and raucous and well liked. You could tell she had a white mother, too, but all it took was one good "innit" to know Carrie belonged in ways I never could. Besides, her hurricane of a personality prohibited certain questions about blood quantum and skin shades.

She'd been on the bus a week. As usual, I

33

kept to myself, hood up, headphones on, straining for invisibility. When the handfuls of pennies smattered against my head, I was only shocked for a moment. Her laugh was unmistakable, her sugary voice spitting "white girl" like fire. Her pale jester face — somehow swept of all irony — ducking down every time I turned around.

That's when it became clear: whiteness meant different things in different contexts. On the rez, Carrie and I could share skin colours and still be perceived entirely differently as Native people. While my culture was derived solely from Michael Jackson videos and Disney's dubious visions of femininity, Carrie's culture was slowly, carefully poured into her hands the same way generations of Six Nations people had culture poured into theirs. It didn't matter that I never chose to be born in Buffalo and raised generically American; that's just the way it was. Eventually there was nothing for me to do but sit there, let the pennies ricochet off my head and hope my non-reaction would make Carrie bored instead of incensed.

5 The day my kid was born, the powwow was rained out. All the spectators and dancers made for the lacrosse arena, leaving

Chiefswood Park soggy and deserted. I hated those arena powwows. I hated that my boyfriend Mike's first powwow was one of those powwows. The experience wasn't right without the dancers blurring against the grass like rushed strokes of paint, haggling over beaded jewellery I couldn't afford, dribbling Indian taco grease onto my shirt and giggling as white visitors claimed their great-great-great-grandmother was a Cherokee princess.

It had been eleven days since my due date and I'd been having irregular contractions for the past two. My dad and brothers were away on a month-long Unity Run, culling my support system down to a skeleton crew. I wondered whether my dad's absence had anything to do with my staunch biological dismissal of his many "marry Native, have Native babies" speeches. Before he left he reminded me my child wouldn't have a status card, that Mike wouldn't be allowed to live on the reserve. I'd rolled my eyes, all eighteen-year-old panache.

My water broke. When we arrived at the birthing centre, my midwife took control, not even balking at my insistence that Coldplay's *Parachutes* soundtrack the next twelve hours. As the labour progressed, though, my father's family history began prowling in the back of my mind. I hadn't given it much thought until then. I thought of his mother, the only one in her family who *didn't* go to residential school, leaving her Six Nations home for Buffalo so her children, too, could bypass the Mush Hole. His older brother murdered by a white bartender over ten dollars. His father murdered by two white men in a roadside scuffle. He himself beaten to a bloodied mass by a white man with a baseball bat at a bar. His was a family legacy that often changed forms. One day it appeared as a six-pack of Bud Light, another as white fingers squeezing a trigger. Sometimes it struck with such violence its only consolation was that it was over quickly; other times it snuck up, draining a life one excruciating drop at a time.

Then my kid came barrelling out of me. Once their complexion settled from the red shock of newborn skin to soft pink, my anxiety abated. Any visible traces of their Native heritage had been blotted out. They didn't even have the brown eyes I'd considered my family's defining trait; squinting from between blond lashes were two splashes of indigo. As much as it made me sick to admit it, internalized racism had warped me so much that I was actually relieved that my child didn't look like my father, my aunts, my uncle, my grandmother. In a better world, one that didn't treat my dark-skinned relatives with violence and indignity and death for the way they looked, I would have been able to long for my child to have the thick, black hair and deep-brown skin my family members have without feeling fear. I would have been able to be disappointed that I didn't see visible reminders of my family line peeking through in my child. I wanted to be able to be disappointed. At that time, in this world, I wasn't. I knew those eyes, that skin, had given them a shield when they could have been a target. Now my kid could, if they chose, deflect the sharp, parasitic legacy of shame and violence they'd inherited and disappear into whiteness. I'd been given the same shield, the same opportunity. I'd never had any of the experiences my father's family had. I probably never would.

But at the same time, while my baby's whiteness gave them a shield, it also erected a barricade between them and their people. They didn't look like kin; they looked like an enemy. If they were on the rez, would they be seen as Mohawk? Or would they be treated as just another white person on a poverty tour? Holding my baby for the first time surrounded by loving, Indigenous midwives, I remembered the pain of passing. The way you deny parts of yourself to appease others, as though identity were so easily partitioned. This day with these people you're Native, while this day with these people you're white. Everything will be fine. You will be fine, ducking in and out of labels with a smile pasted on. All the guilt any white person feels for centuries of racial genocide and injustice welled up in me. But it was more complicated than that: I was both the winner and the loser, the victim and the abuser. Two strains married in me, impossibly. Any time I felt outrage at something a white person said or did to my people, I felt like a fraud, as if I, too, were culpable. Yet if a Native person made a sweeping statement about white people, I couldn't help but question my belonging. After all, I didn't have enough knowledge of my culture to mitigate my skin colour. Defences were always up. The tear always widening.

When my father talked about the issues our people faced, he uttered a three-word mantra as the solution: decolonizing the mind. He was referring to a process of retraining one's brain to reject the values of Western culture. Or, in his words, "to stop living in the boat, and come back to the canoe." That solution fell flat for me. Born from both the boat and the canoe, I'd always felt I didn't belong in either, so I was left drowning in between.

Maybe being mixed-race doesn't have to mean shaming myself out of my Indigeneity just because I wasn't raised in the culture: silently, safely watching from my whiteness as Native people around me suffered. Maybe it doesn't have to feel like forcing a smile for the same white people who continually gut my community and myself with dull blades.

This is how I can decolonize my mind: by refusing the colonial narratives that try to keep me alienated from my own community. I can raise my kid to love being Haudenosaunee in a way my parents couldn't, in a way my grandparents couldn't. This is my responsibility as a Haudenosaunee woman.

But my white-passing privilege gives me another, more complex responsibility. I have to use my white privilege like an undercover agent would use a good disguise, leveraging my lightness to drop the guard of non-Indigenous people around me, then slowly, methodically picking at their inherited colonialism, forcing them to re-evaluate their own complicity in a way they may not have if they could easily identify me as Indigenous. More importantly, I need to lift up the voices of those in my community who, like my uncle, like my grandfather, like my father, are treated as less than human, unworthy of attention or time, because their skin is too dark for certain people's liking. I need to make sure that their experiences are centred, that their concerns are heard, that their needs are met.

Being both Haudenosaunee and white wasn't a curse meant to tear me in two; it was a call to uphold the different responsibilities that came with each part of me. Turns out my dad was wrong. I didn't need to worry about whether to get in the boat or the canoe, and I certainly didn't need to drown in between. Understanding and honouring my unique responsibilities was always the way to keep myself afloat.

On Seeing and Being Seen

I've heard that when you see someone you love your pupils get bigger, as if your eyes themselves want to swallow them up and trap them inside. I don't know if that same physiology applies to seeing objects, but I like to imagine my pupils were huge, hungry black orbs when I first read Michi Saagiig Nishnaabeg writer, activist and teacher Leanne Betasamosake Simpson's *Islands of Decolonial Love*. Every sentence felt like a fingertip strumming a neglected chord in my life, creating the most gorgeous music I'd ever heard.

It was the first time I, an Indigenous woman, had read the work of another Indigenous woman. It was such an intimate and personally revelatory moment — as if she had reached out from the pages, lifted my face and smiled. *She can see me,* I thought. *She can see me.* I was twenty-five years old.

I'd known I wanted to write since I was twelve, but back then I'd never seen a girl like myself in the books I loved so much. I saw white girls — often upper middle class, often pining after unremarkable white boys. So that's what I wrote. I wrote my way out of used clothes and food banks and parents who screamed in the night. None of my characters ever worried about money. None of them were concerned what their friends would think if they met their Haudeno-saunee dad or their white bipolar mother. None of them even *had* a Haudenosaunee dad or white bipolar mother. Things were simple; things were normal. Rich boys and brand names were normal.

My taste in literature changed as I got older. What didn't change was my suspicion that publishers felt Indigenous girls like me were unworthy of book covers or book deals. Even in university the writers we studied were white: Margaret Atwood, Alice Munro, Jane Austen. I admired the work of these women, but they weren't writing what I needed to read, and this made it hard to believe there was space for what I needed to write.

So imagine my surprise when a fellow writer — a white woman — told me during post-workshop beers that I was going to get published right away because I was Native. We were in the same undergraduate creative writing classes together. We'd had to apply to the program the year before with 25 pages of poetry and fiction. Less than a dozen writers were accepted. That first year my fiction included one short story about a white woman with a mixed-race child and the beginning of a novel about three generations of Indigenous women. I was particularly excited about the novel, about the possibility of writing Native women like the ones I knew, and the workshop feedback was enthusiastic. Still, this white woman — who wrote effusive comments on all my work — had determined that my talent was not enough to get me published. Only my ethnicity could do that. The funny thing was, I could count the Native writers I knew of with half a hand — none of whom were women, and none of whom were writing about Native women in a way I recognized.

The idea that the colonialism, racism and sexism that had systematically kept Indigenous women out of the literary community could somehow be leveraged to benefit me as an Indigenous woman through some half-assed literary affirmative action was absurd. And yet this white woman believed it with her whole heart. This white woman, who one year later got into an MFA program with scholarships while I was rejected from every one I applied to. Perhaps I hadn't made it clear enough on the application that I was Native. Perhaps I had made it too clear on the application I was Native. It was hard to say.

I stopped writing for years after those rejections. When I did write — between being a mother and shifts at my minimum-wage job — I scraped all Indigeneity out of my work. At least if my fiction read as "white" I'd be sure that any rejections were based on the work itself. I wouldn't have to field questions about why my characters were Native, or deal with criticisms that they somehow weren't "Indian enough" — issues that, as far as I could tell, never came up for white writers, for white work.

Then came *Islands of Decolonial Love.* Everything changed. Reading stories of Indigenous women who had good sex and bad boyfriends, who dealt with both underhanded and overt racism, who spoke their language and loved their families, gave me hope. Here — in these pages — was what I'd been searching for my whole life. Finally, after twenty-five years, I felt there was space for me to breathe inside the claustrophobic world of white Western literature. Reading

Simpson's stories ultimately gave me permission to write my own.

Of course, this didn't change the realities of the publishing industry. I once entered a short story contest with a piece about a complicated relationship between two Indigenous women and lost to a story written by a white American man that not only appropriated but outright misrepresented Indigenous ceremonies. His story featured stereotypical drunken, dysfunctional Indians, one of whom offered his white girlfriend — the story's protagonist, naturally — to his brother during potlatch. His brother accepted, and the two went off and had sex in the woods, the rest of the Natives vomiting and partying around them.

Potlatch ceremonies had to be held in secret from 1885 until 1951 because they were banned by the Canadian government. There was a raid on the B.C. village of Memkumlis in 1921, and forty-five people performing potlatch were arrested. Twenty of those arrested were sent to prison. I shudder to think of how their grandchildren would react if they read this story and saw how the powerful ceremony their ancestors fought for was turned into racist, colonial poverty porn. The old questions emerged: Was this, a story written by a white man in another country, more "Indian" than my own writing as an Indigenous woman? Did this racist portrayal and cultural appropriation of Indigenous people matter if the story was otherwise "good"?

That is the crucial problem with the push for "diversity" in publishing — something I've known my whole life but have only recently been able to articulate. "Diversity" is not about letting those who aren't white make whatever art matters to them and their communities. If that were the case, it would not have taken me twenty-five years to find a book that represented Indigenous women in a meaningful way.

No, "diversity," as Tania Canas so succinctly puts it in her essay "Diversity is a White Word," is about making sense of difference "through the white lens . . . by creating, curating and demanding palatable definitions of 'diversity' but only in relation to what this means in terms of whiteness." It's the literary equivalent of "ethnic" restaurants: they please white people because they provide them with "exotic" new flavours, but if they don't appease white people's sensitive taste buds they're not worth a damn.

White authors writing from other racial perspectives is hardly new. As early as 1893,

Mohawk writer Pauline Johnson criticized how white writers portrayed Native women. Back then, countless white authors — particularly men — wrote the "Indian maiden" trope: Native women so hopelessly in love with white men that they were willing to betray their nation to help the men achieve their goals. When this did not win the love of these dashing white men, as it almost never did — for what white man in his right mind would love a Native woman when white women were available? — the heartbroken Indian maidens would commit suicide. In her *Toronto Sunday Globe* editorial "A Strong Race Opinion," Johnson called out these writers for their ignorance:

Perhaps, sometimes an Indian romance may be written by someone who will be clever enough to portray national character without ever coming in contact with it. . . . But such things are rare, half of our authors who write up Indian stuff have never been on an Indian reserve in their lives, have never met a "real live" Redman . . . ; what wonder that their conception of a people that they are ignorant of, save by hear-say, is dwarfed, erroneous and delusive.

Johnson could very well have been describing the white man who, a hundred and twenty years later, wrote that contest-winning story about potlatch. Research into Indigenous life is not necessary because these writers are not writing real Indigenous people; they are writing Indigenous stereotypes that their white readers recognize and falsely consider authentic.

Perhaps these white writers believe, as my classmate did, that Black writers, Indigenous writers and other writers of colour have an edge in the current publishing climate, and as a result, white writers must now make their texts more "diverse" to compete. Johnson made a similar argument back in 1893: "Do [non-Native] authors who write Indian romances love the nation they endeavour successfully or unsuccessfully to describe? . . . or is the Indian introduced into literature but to lend a dash of vivid colouring to an otherwise tame and sombre picture of colonial life?" These questions remain pertinent for white writers to answer. Yet it would seem those are exactly the questions they want to avoid.

I will not say that these authors cannot write from an experience they've never had. To an extent, all fiction writers write from experiences they've never had, since the characters they're writing aren't real. However, there is a marked difference between the way the man who wrote the potlatch story wrote Indigenous people and the way Leanne Betasamosake Simpson writes Indigenous people. What is that difference? Well, there is this oft-cited notion that you can write from any perspective as long as you write with empathy. I don't know whether the white man who wrote about the potlatch felt he was writing with empathy. He may have. He might have no idea why his words were offensive to me. He could even read this essay and liken my criticism of his work to censorship.

That was British author Lionel Shriver's reaction in September 2016 to a review of her novel *The Mandibles.* In the review, (white) writer Ken Kalfus of *The Washington Post* said Shriver's Black and Latinx characters were "racist characterizations." The Black woman in *The Mandibles* has dementia and is either restrained or led around on a leash by her white husband. The Latinx character is a pudgy, lisping Mexican-born man who uses lax immigration laws and constitutional amendments to become America's "criminally incompetent" president. Instead of asking herself questions similar to those Johnson posed, or considering Kalfus's criticism, Shriver wrote a speech complaining about "fiction and identity politics" and delivered it at the Brisbane Writers Festival. In it, she claimed people concerned about inaccurate representations and cultural appropriation in fiction were stifling free speech. Of course, that's the knee-jerk reaction many white people have when marginalized communities criticize them: criticism magically becomes censorship. Who knows? Maybe Shriver thought she was writing with empathy, too.

But writing with empathy is not enough. It never has been. Depictions like these — reactions like these — are proof that white people are willing to extend only so much empathy to those who aren't white. Empathy has its limits — and, contrary to what some may think, it is possible to both have empathy for a person and still hold inherited, unacknowledged racist views about them and their worth. How else do you explain the Canadian government's apology for residential schools and pleas for reconciliation coexisting with its continued, purposeful underfunding of Indigenous children? How do you take the U.S. government's 2009 apology for "violence, maltreatment and neglect inflicted on Native Peoples" seriously when the wording of that very apology refuses any and all legal and financial liability? How do you come to understand a country that expressed outrage when a white woman murdered pregnant twenty-two-year-old Choctaw woman Savanna LaFontaine-Greywind, cutting out and stealing her baby in the process, at the same time the president of that country and his legions of supporters continued to mockingly refer to his (white) political opponent Elizabeth Warren as "Pocahontas"? Clearly having empathy is not dependent upon understanding the social, political and historical circumstances that made that empathy necessary in the first place. And yet we continue to expect empathy alone to create change, as though empathy would rethink our priorities, rewrite our laws and restructure our society for us.

To truly write from another experience in an authentic way, you need more than empathy. You need to write with love. *That* is what I felt when I read Simpson's stories. That's what I feel when I read the work of Gwen Benaway, Waubgeshig Rice, Louise Erdrich, Joy Harjo, Tracey Lindberg, Eden Robinson, Katherena Vermette, Elissa Washuta, Billy-Ray Belcourt, Joshua Whitehead, Lindsay Nixon, Terese Marie Mailhot

51

and Cherie Dimaline. That's what I hope Indigenous people feel when they read my work. Love.

Love pushes us to believe, even when reason tells us we should stop. Love compels us to move carefully, to consider the consequences of our actions. Love reminds us what's worth fighting for, what isn't. Love begs us to stop being passive and finally act.

If you can't write about us with a love for who we are as a people, what we've survived, what we've accomplished despite all attempts to keep us from doing so; if you can't look at us as we are and feel your pupils go wide, rendering all stereotypes a sham, a poor copy, a disgrace — then why are you writing about us at all?

WEIGHT

You know as soon as it happens, feel it like a tiny pebble settling in your uterus. This directly contradicts your tenth grade health class, which claimed it takes days, not seconds, for implantation, but the Catholic paranoia you've inherited from your mother is far stronger than logic.

Another thing you were supposed to have learned in tenth grade health class: strategic ways to say no to men you imagined as mustachioed villains from silent films, tying women to railroad tracks between exaggerated title cards. You never imagined having to say no to real boys. Your femininity was safely bundled beneath cheap, ill-fitting sweaters and baggy jeans, a veritable Do Not Enter sign you hoped would keep out the unworthy. You certainly didn't expect to have to say no to *the boy,* the one you'd been pining after since tenth grade, inspiring you to obsessively scribble "MIKE +

ALICIA" on the wooden slats that held up your sister's top bunk. Yet here you were: in a lukewarm, year-long relationship frequently punctuated by your sighs and his silence.

You wanted to say no to him that night, but despite your Ontario curriculum training, you weren't really sure how, so you reluctantly agreed. It was quick, awkward and silent, surrounded by sleeping boys you barely knew who were there for Mike's birthday party. Even though there was no Hallelujah choir or moment of transcendence, there was still a minor thrill in finally doing something your Catholic mother disapproved of. That was sort of an achievement.

Your high school is called PJ, which stands for Pauline Johnson, the local Mohawk poet good enough to name a school after but apparently not good enough to have her work taught within it. Students at rival high schools use the initials quite differently, though, referring to you and your classmates as "Pregnant Juveniles." The nickname's an unfortunate, if predictable, side effect of being the only high school sensible enough to offer a daycare in the teen-pregnancy capital of Canada. All the knocked-up teens in Brantford get shuttled here, stretch marks peeking out of their low-rise jeans, strollers stowed away in their lockers. You used to look down on those girls. Now you're sure you can feel your organs shifting inside as you walk down the halls. You wonder if that's how those girls felt, too, as their lower abdomens pushed into that telltale pear shape and whispers grew to a hum.

Mike doesn't mention it, but you know he's worried, too. He'll sometimes lean in close after friends leave and ask if you're in the clear yet. You press your lips together, make a light-hearted joke.

Whenever you're alone, you place an anxious hand on your belly, feeling for a fluttering heartbeat. You've heard throwing yourself down the stairs can cause miscarriage. But stairs are in short supply when you live in a trailer on the rez. You wonder whether jumping from your half-metre-high porch would do the trick, but quickly conclude its accident-causing capabilities end at a sprained ankle.

It's been a month and still no blood. You watch as the school bus carrying your sister barrels back to the rez, then catch a city bus to the walk-in clinic. You haven't had any symptoms — no breast soreness, no fatigue, no nausea or vomiting — yet you know that tiny weight is there: unmoving, but alive.

You whisper to the receptionist what you need. The room is too small for secrets. Other patients' ears perk up and they give you the once-over, sure the uncertain state of your uterus tells them all they need to know about you.

"Ten dollars," the receptionist says. You must look confused because her eyebrows arch. "For the test."

You fish a purple bill from the small yellow envelope in your purse. You wait.

Eventually a man leads you into a room and asks you to pee into a clear container, which is slightly alarming since you've never seen it happen this way in movies. Then again, teenage sex doesn't lead to pregnancy in most movies, either.

You wait some more. Though there's still no proof it's even there, you feel that tiny pebble of a person inside you so acutely: a little anchor docking you to the reserve. With every passing minute, this future that was supposed to belong to someone else — some cheap-beer-guzzling party girl with no aspiration to do anything but keep her small waistline and have a good time — takes solid shape before you. It doesn't matter that you took conscious effort to make yourself unfeminine, that you maintain a self-imposed standard of sobriety, that you have plans to become a famous writer immediately upon graduation. All your potential, all your plans, will remain just that: frozen by time and circumstance. You'll continue to work an under-the-table job, lead an under-the-table life. This is how statistics are born.

The man returns, confirming what you've known for weeks. He offers no comment or congratulations. You're thankful for this.

You wait to cry until you're back on the bus. No one notices your quaking shoulders, your muted sobs.

If you were in a silent movie right now the title card would ask the most teenage of all questions: *"Why me?"*

The woman in front of you looks like the lead from *Touched by an Angel*. Red hair, pale skin, perpetually wounded. Last week this woman gave you a small book with purple lilacs on the cover. It was presented as a pregnant teen's diary, but it was written by a middle-aged woman with a poor grasp of slang and an even worse grasp of grammar. As you read you made revisions in bright blue pen.

The woman asks if you liked it. You pause. What she really wants to ask is whether you're considering abortion, which the "diary" has implied is a moral decision on par with blowing up a hospital. You're not sure if on-the-spot exorcisms are a thing, but you suspect this woman could arrange one for the very disturbed or the very feminist. You cautiously observe that the book was "okay."

She moves on, asking about your family history while Mike sits beside you, shifting uncomfortably. You wonder how many other good, confirmed Catholic girls she's interrogated like this, how many families she's boiled down to a series of checkmarks on a page for the casual perusal of the childless. So far your family has become diabetes, cancer, alcoholism, drug addiction, cerebral palsy, mental illness.

"What kind of mental illness?" the woman asks, leaning forward. "It's important we're specific so" — her voice drops a register — "the family knows." *The family.* She says it with such ominous singularity it calls to mind the mafia.

You glance uneasily at Mike. He doesn't know this part yet. No one does, really. You don't remember being outright told to keep it secret. Repression was learned in your household as coolly as vocal tics or table manners. You didn't even whisper about it with your sister at night between bunks, and you whispered with her about everything.

"What kind of mental illness, Alicia?"

"Bipolar disorder." The words tumble strange and unpractised from your mouth. These words, this diagnosis, is supposed to explain away your mother's erratic presence in your life. It seems unfair that so much pain can be summed up so succinctly. Her illness — its stranglehold — feels much bigger than six syllables.

It usually happens like this: your mother gets really sad or really angry, and some days when you come home from school she's gone. After a month or two, she reappears just as suddenly, smiling and shiny and normal. And no one talks about it. Then two or three months later the hospital cycle starts back up again, and again, you find yourself the de facto mother of four confused siblings — cooking cheap, unfortunate dinners, changing diapers during *Buffy the Vampire Slayer*'s commercial breaks.

"Do you know what kind? There are different types . . ."

"I don't know." Your voice shakes. You clench your jaw and stare at the spot directly between the woman's eyebrows, trying not to blink. Her pores are larger than yours, but smaller than your mother's. Everything about your mother is big: her voice, her smile, her mood swings, her devotion to the

59

Catholic Church, her love.

She cried even harder than you did when she found out. Not that you delivered the news with much finesse. In the midst of a fight with both parents, you screamed, "By the way, I'm pregnant!" just before slamming the trailer door and stomping down the driveway to a waiting cab.

Since then, you've heard her mutter about sin repeating itself when she thinks you can't hear. Or maybe when she thinks you can. Her big sin was having three kids out of wedlock before marrying your father. As her own personal penance, she forced Catholicism on you and your siblings with an almost supernatural zeal. But all the rosaries in the world couldn't curb teenage hormones or your pathological desire to please. Like mother, like daughter.

"Is it in your immediate family?" the woman asks.

"Yes, it's my mom. Can we please stop talking about it now?" Your face is hot. Your mom's sitting outside this windowless room right now, probably clutching one of the many wrinkled tissues she keeps stowed in her purse, smelling of pressed powder.

The woman smiles, leans further forward, places her hand on your knee the way all women like this presume they're allowed to place hands on a stranger's knees.

"I know this is hard for you and I don't want to pry —" *Stop the sentence there,* you think. *Just stop.* "But we need to know how many generations back the bipolar goes. The family needs to know what they're getting themselves into. That type of disease is genetic."

You first learned about genetics in eighth grade. Dominant and recessive genes. Chromosomes and DNA. You even did probability charts to determine what your potential kids might look like. All of it seemed exceedingly superficial. Who really cared if their baby had brown eyes instead of blue? Curly hair or straight?

Until now, it never occurred to you that genes could be toxic, planting illness like landmines in your child. One false step and your child's brain — your child's life — could become bloodied pulp. You think of your mother and her stop-start-stop-start life. Is she really happy? Does she remember what she does when she's in the throes of her illness? The names she calls you when she's manic? The times she's been catatonic, too depressed to even speak? Late one night, shortly after she got back from the hospital, you remember her telling your dad about being strapped to a bed. She was in

61

the restraints for hours, screaming and crying. Eventually she wet herself. She relayed the details calmly, clinically, as though they belonged to someone else. Your father said nothing. You were starting to think he'd left the room until you heard his voice, all thunder and annoyance. He was trying to watch TV.

The memories rise unbidden, and it's as if your body explodes. There is no working up to it, no slow progression of emotion. You're hysterical: face now red with tears, breaths now hiccuping gasps.

The woman fumbles for a box of tissues as she stutters her apologies. You realize all at once you hate her. She's the type of woman who, a handful of decades ago, would have carted your dad's aunts and uncles off to residential schools without batting an eye.

Then Mike tells the woman to stop. His sentences are short and incontestable. Like the love interest in a John Hughes movie, he stands, grabs your hand and leads you out of the room, then out of the building.

Apart from the teen pregnancy and the hyperventilating, you think this is probably the most romantic thing that's ever happened to you.

There are so few differences between idealism and arrogance. You thought it would be easy to be a full-time student and a part-time mother, coming home on weekends to nurse your baby and kiss your baby and try to convince them they're still *your* baby between reading strange novels and writing eight-page essays. You thought it would be easy to integrate with your classmates, building lifelong friendships with students as eager and hungry and curious as you are.

Instead, you've replaced silence about your own mother with silence about being a mother — a decision that leaves you mute, marooned in small talk and superficiality. Everyone on your residence floor seems to be friends except you. You don't watch *Grey's Anatomy* in the common room; you don't complain about unfair professors or restrictive meal plans. If this were a movie, you'd be an extra. Scenery, even.

Not that you want to be friendless. You just know that if you were to explain your situation to anyone, you'd compulsively search faces, analyzing lip twitches and forehead creases, tracking judgment like a bloodhound tracks game. It doesn't matter that your floor has a co-ed bathroom and you've heard so many of their drunken hookups that you're starting to recognize them by their coital grunts. That type of shame is normal. They are normal. Your shame is not. You are not.

The one benefit to having almost no friends is you don't have to make excuses to run back to your dorm room and pump breast milk. Every four hours you're back in your bedroom with a glorified suction cup, watching white drops trickle into a bottle, the contents of which you pour into a Ziploc bag, seal on all sides with masking tape and pop into the freezer. At first the milk comes easily; you're done in fifteen minutes flat. But the longer you're away from your baby, the longer it takes. Soon it takes an episode and a half of *Veronica Mars* to pump a measly four ounces. Your frozen haul shrinks considerably. Mike's mother still brags about your dedication, as if you're some lactating folk hero, but you've noticed opened tins of Similac on her counter. The only thing you alone can provide for your kid can be replaced for $24.95 at most shopping centres.

One day your gender studies class is discussing Toni Morrison's *Beloved*–specifically, the scene where Sethe kills her two-year-old daughter rather than return her to a life of slavery. You remain silent as you listen to your classmates (all of whom are young and childless, all of whom are white) debate Sethe's actions. What kind of mother does that to her child? What kind of mother would want her child to be born into a life like that? Bad mother, bad mother, bad mother.

Suddenly, your professor declares that mothers are the most hated group of people in the world. He doesn't elaborate, he just lets the statement sit. Your stomach churns as you glance around at similarly slack-jawed students. Despite the looks of confusion, and the general tendency for university students to argue, no one protests. Not even you.

You mull over this statement for weeks. Your own mother was the stay-at-home mom to seven kids in total, though one of them chose to live with your grandmother after a custody battle and another was disabled, with very little control over her muscles, so your mother put her in a home where they could provide round-the-clock care. You're not sure how much of any of that was her choice. Since she's been married, she's been in and out of hospitals too often to hold down a job. On top of that, she has the inglorious distinction of being one of the few white illegal aliens on Six Nations. If anyone reports her to band council, she'll be not only kicked off the reserve but deported. Her options have never really been options at all.

Still, for over a decade of your life, if she was ever tired or annoyed or depressed or manic, your childish brain conveniently edited that out, preferring to preserve her as an ever-smiling, ever-fertile saint. This delusion was so strong, in fact, that until you were twelve you wanted to be a stay-at-home mom, too. You imagined a motley crew of children shrieking on the lawn and tugging at your legs and holding up their arms to you in near-holy reverie. You, their blessed mother.

Of course your own blessed mother didn't live just for you. She taught herself computer languages, researched the latest advances in technology, wrote up elaborate business plans and promised you wild wealth would be yours within a year. But she could only ever do those things when you and your siblings were at school. As soon as any of you got home, the battle for her undivided attention began. Your brother would climb on her lap and strategically position his face in front of the computer monitor, moving his head to match hers whenever she tried to look around him. Your sister would thrust tests and homework in her face, ask pointed questions, then cry over her one-syllable responses. You would whine about how she never really listened to you anymore, as though her ability to absorb middle-school gossip trumped her attempts to program your family out of poverty. At that time, at that age, it did. None of you hated your mother, but none of you acknowledged she was her own person, either. Isn't that its own sort of hatred? Isn't that why you won't tell anyone about the child you left behind?

Though Mike is sympathetic and supportive, he doesn't seem to feel nearly as guilty as you do. He still seems whole. You watch movies together, you cuddle, you load into your father's van and drive to his mother's house to see your baby on Friday nights. Though everyone back home asks you about your child, no one ever asks him about his.

When you get back to Mike's mom's crowded apartment your baby is asleep. You know that they're a light sleeper, that you should leave them alone, but it's such a perfect moment. You bend down and kiss their hairline. The wrinkles on their forehead ripple outward, then smooth. For a moment it seems like you're in the clear. Then their eyes burst open and they let loose an unholy howl and you know that you messed up.

But a funny thing happens. Between their cries you hear their tiny warbling voice say a word for the first time. It may be totally accidental, two syllables randomly mashed together, and they may not know what it means and they may only see you on weekends and your milk may have dried up, leaving them with an overpriced instant substitute, but your baby is looking at you now through clotted lashes, calling you Mama.

It's not how you wanted it, but it's enough.

THE SAME SPACE

Every time I come back to Bloor and Lansdowne — the increasingly gentrified Toronto neighborhood where I clumsily stumbled into adulthood — my blood runs a little faster through my veins.

Run through these streets, *my instincts say,* run your fingertips over each brick of each building. Feel the roughness, the sturdiness, the strength. Feel the sun and the particular way it cuts through the trees, warming your neck, your arms, your legs before its unblinking attention becomes too much and you go home sunburnt. Hear the night, which is never totally silent — raccoons hissing or late-night, liquored-up strangers laughing or street sweepers rumbling or delivery trucks beeping while backing up. See the night, see how its darkness always has an escape hatch — a streetlight or lit-up store sign to guide you home, even when the city's radiance blocks out the stars.

Place your hand over this neighbourhood's heart, feel it beat against your palm. Love its perfection. Love its imperfection. Feel home again.

But I'm not home again. Not really. This hasn't been my home for seven years. My brother Mikey, a freshly minted adult, is moving here to go to CMU College of Makeup Artistry and Design. He wants to learn how to transform faces with powders and liquids and brushes and paints — part magician, part alchemist. This neighborhood will be his home soon. I'm not one to necessarily believe in fate, but I can recognize a good coincidence when I see one. This is definitely a coincidence.

As we walk down the familiar streets together — past the Value Village, the Coffee Time, the restaurants drawing us in with scents of curry and coffee and cookies and chicken — I see his eyes go wide with possibility. I'm sure mine did the same back then. I'm sure they're doing the same now. After all, few are immune to the shiny neon and collapsed boundaries of big-city capitalism.

Mikey shows me his apartment. It's small, like mine was, but at least its floors are level. I know he'll push against the smallness, the tightness, assert himself within this space until he feels a sort of cozy comfort in its claustrophobia. Our home on Six Nations was small, too, but we had whole fields of green to explore, thick forests to investigate, a browning creek to stick our toes in or rush across.

Though the green here is mostly confined to small patches around houses, sometimes lounging luxuriously across a handful of parks, in its place lies a different sort of freedom: anonymity. Toronto is so big, this neighbourhood so busy and full, one's personal history gets lost in its frenzy. Back on the rez, both Mikey and I were Wes's kids, the newest links in a chain of history that reached back much farther than anyone ever bothered to explain to us. *But here, among all these people who don't know your name or face or history, you can just be you.* Unbuckle your uncomfortable past, *the city murmurs.* Pack it tight in a box and shove it in the back of your closet. Stretch your newly unburdened shoulders. Choose your own adventure.

I was still in school when I lived here, finishing an English lit degree, taking hour-long transit rides to York University, where I would read and dream my name would one day be boldly printed down book spines, too. I took a class on diaspora literatures, attracted by the elusive promise of actual Indigenous writers on a course syllabus. It was difficult, combining complex theory with complex books. On top of that, my professor was blindingly, intimidatingly smart — the type of person who mercilessly dissected any answer to any question she posed, and therefore terrified everyone into silence for a few seconds whenever she spoke.

"Why do you think I included Indigenous literature in a diaspora course?" she asked one day.

I surprised myself by answering without a second's hesitation. "Because Indigenous people are almost always put in the position where they're displaced on their own lands."

My professor didn't dissect anything. She simply smiled, impressed. I knew I should have felt proud that she approved, and I did, but I also felt a pressure building in my chest — one that perhaps was always there, but hidden away, like my own past.

I'd always been close-lipped about my family life — the violence, the joys, the poverty, the precariousness. Part of this was because my family moved so often. I knew better than to offer the sort of vulnerabilities upon

72

which lifelong friendships are built; I was only going to move again, anyway. The other reason was that I knew that my family wasn't a normal, charming, made-for-TV type of dysfunctional. We were the type of dysfunctional where the police could be called on our parents, by our parents; where social services could be knocking on our door if we said the wrong thing to a teacher, or even if we didn't say anything at all, as though there were some sort of aura hanging around us that everyone identified as wrong.

How could a seven-year-old explain any of this to another seven-year-old? A fourteen-year-old to a fourteen-year-old? An eighteen-year-old to an eighteen-year-old? I can't even write this now without feeling like I have to make excuses for my family, to explain that despite all the dysfunction and trauma, each of my siblings was raised with so much love and self-confidence that we're all now, as adults, doing well in our chosen fields, and even if we weren't, we still deserve to be considered more than our dysfunction and trauma, we still deserve to be considered valuable, whole.

Instead of attempting to explain any of this to any friends, I learned how to fake intimacy. Turned out that as long as you were funny and fun, people would want to spend time with you; as long as you were willing to listen to their problems, they didn't notice you weren't telling them any of your own. I knew so much about my friends. They knew almost nothing about me. This was how I created a double life: no matter how awful things were at home, I could go to school and, from nine to three, pretend that nothing at all was wrong. But once 3:01 hit and I got on the bus home, I could no longer stop myself from wondering what awaited me when I got off.

There was a problem with this strategy that I didn't anticipate. The longer I went without talking to my friends about my problems, the harder it was to talk to them when I actually needed to. If I had slowly unspooled my life for them, as they had for me, they would be prepared when something particularly difficult came up. They would already know the context. Now, if I wanted to talk to them about anything, I would have to explain everything — all the truth I'd tried so hard to keep from everyone. I had no idea how to go about that, so instead I just continued on as I always had: the girl without a family or past, who you could always rely on to keep all your secrets because she kept her own so well.

■ ■ ■

This is not the same neighbourhood I left all those years ago. Time passes and spaces change, whether you're there to witness it or not. Here, at Bloor and Lansdowne, gentrification is now in full swing. Bloor West is now the proud owner of shiny new vegan bakeries and boutique cafés — ventures that seemed unthinkable when these streets held me close. A few restaurants and businesses have already abandoned the area, the trendiness they helped create now turning on them, pricing them out.

In Leslie Jamison's essay "Fog Count," she goes to visit a friend in prison and, while there, realizes her experience of the prison as a visitor will never be the same as his as an inmate: "The truth is we never occupied the same space. A space isn't the same for a person who has chosen to be there and a person who hasn't." Jamison can ask as many probing questions as she wants, can write down all the details, but she will always, in effect, be a tourist in that space because she can always choose to leave.

I wonder if the people who are choosing to bring money into this neighbourhood, choosing to paint over its poverty, swat away its seediness, transform it into something shiny, clean and appealing to upper-middle-class families, recognize they, too, are tourists, inviting in more tourists to take advantage of its low rent and subway access, encouraging them to make homes where homes were already made. They see the neighbourhood as a big red X on a treasure map, and, shovel in hand, are determined to mine its bounty from beneath the beds of the natives. Meanwhile, those who live here because they have to, who have always made the most of what they've begrudgingly been given, are now being told that their achievements in this space are not enough, that they haven't used the space properly, haven't realized its "potential," and must leave to make room for "progress." They see the neighbourhood as their home — a space that already has inherent worth, whether outsiders recognize that worth or not.

Or, as Jamison might say, the same space, but also not the same at all.

In my diaspora class we often talked about the experience of diaspora: remembering your past in your former home and constantly measuring it against your present in your current home, knowing you can never again re-enter the time and space you left, knowing you have lost access to that possible future forever, knowing your home will change without you, knowing you will change without your home — and knowing, in some instances, none of that was your choice.

Jamison wasn't exactly right. There aren't only two ways to consider a place. It isn't just about those who choose to be there and those who don't. What about those who had never chosen *not* to be there? What about those who were forced out?

Tucked away in a box at the back of this city's closet is a history. The history is this: Toronto was once Tkaronto. This city ruled by bylaws was once ruled by treaty. It was what my people call Dish With One Spoon territory: a space that was shared by the Haudenosaunee, the Mississaugas of the New Credit, the Anishinaabe, the Huron, the Wendat. This land was not supposed to have its plenty mined and discarded; it was supposed to be treated as one collective dish each nation had to share, hunting an equal but sustainable amount of game. All would eat from that dish together, using a beaver tail spoon instead of a knife to ensure there was no accidental bloodshed — which might lead to intentional bloodshed. In this way, it was a space of mutual peace and prosperity.

But early settlers approached the land with the eyes of enterprising tourists: looking at its green, its forests, its waters — and seeing a big red X. They forced out the lands' native inhabitants and went about realizing this land's "potential," laying roads and constructing buildings, later putting up condos and converting old restaurants into cafés.

It was the same space, but also not the same at all.

Before Bloor West had a chance to push me out, Six Nations pulled me back in. That box at the back of my own closet, that box holding my history tight, that I hadn't opened for anyone my entire life, wouldn't stop whispering to me. *Don't forget,* it said. *Don't forget like this city forgot. Don't make the same mistakes this city keeps making.*

While I was taking a fiction and creative nonfiction course in my last year of university, my past started to overwhelm my work. It was as though all the things I didn't know how to say out loud were storming the page, well past ready to finally be articulated. After all those years of forcing my past behind a dam, the pieces I was writing were like a flood. Readers weren't invited in so much as they were drowned, carried by the tide of my trauma to endings that felt like gasps for air. One friend told me an essay I'd written as a letter to my mother made her feel incredibly uncomfortable, like she shouldn't be reading it. In a way, she was right. She shouldn't have been reading it. It wasn't so much a piece of creative nonfiction as it was an exorcism. If no one could handle how intense that was, fine. I needed to figure out how to talk about my past the only way I could: by writing it.

No trace of Indigenous history is etched into these sidewalks, illuminated by these streetlights, cemented between these bricks — not when I lived here years ago, and not today. That past is still packed up, forgotten. Descendants of this land's original caretakers are still here, though. We're laughing with our friends outside the movie theatre, or trying to get by selling dreamcatchers from fleece blankets arranged carefully on big city sidewalks, or dancing in our regalia at powwows we've been anticipating for weeks, or reading on the subway on the way to school. We're here, in diaspora on our own lands. We're watching as the same exploitive process that pushed our people out centuries ago continues to push out others today — an updated version with different copyrights attached.

Whenever I visit my brother, I'll walk the streets of Bloor and Lansdowne and remember what it felt like to finally be able to talk openly about my past. How I felt a relief I'd never known until then, because I could finally be seen for who I was, known for who I was, loved for who I was. I'll observe the neighbourhood with the warm nostalgia and cool distance of a former lover: measuring the present against the past, frowning at disappointing changes, smiling at positive ones, ultimately hopeful. *Perhaps one day this neighbourhood, this city, this country, will finally hear its neglected past whispering,* Look at me plainly. Look at me. Look at your patterns. Don't make the same mistakes. Don't hide who you were. Acknowledge it, then make something new, something beautiful, something that will make everyone proud.

Dark Matters

To say dark matter was "discovered" is disingenuous since, theoretically, dark matter has always been here, filling space we once thought of as empty. In that way it's not so different from these lands, which my father's people refer to as Turtle Island and my mother's people refer to as North America. To this day, people claim the Americas were "discovered" in 1492, despite people living on these lands, creating on these lands, building histories on these lands for centuries before Columbus ambled along. Approximately one-fifth of the world's human population made their home on Turtle Island at the time, not including all the species of plants, animals, birds and fish those people cared for. It takes a certain kind of arrogance to assume that an entire continent didn't exist before you chose to see it.

■ ■ ■ ■

My family and I had just sat down in a Starbucks when I found out. I opened Twitter, looked at my mentions. An acquaintance had tagged me and a number of Indigenous people I knew. Three words were written at the end of the list: "I'm so sorry." Nothing more needed to be said. I knew at that moment white Saskatchewan farmer Gerald Stanley had been found innocent of all charges related to his killing of twenty-two-year-old nêhiyaw man Colten Boushie.

There's never a good time to get news that breaks you, but sitting in a Starbucks with your family in the midst of a vacation seems particularly inopportune. My husband and child were visiting Vancouver while I was on a fellowship at a major university. We'd visited the Contemporary Art Gallery that day. The main exhibit, "Two Scores," was split between rooms. In the first room were Vancouver artist Brent Wadden's giant woven blankets, which he apparently insists on calling "paintings." They lacked the artistry of the Squamish weavings we'd seen a few days before at the Museum of Anthropology. The gallery write-up, however, spun this messiness into a positive, describing

Wadden's self-taught weavings as "exploratory . . . purposefully naïve" — even if they were "often inefficient . . . [and] would confound a traditionally-trained practitioner." I wondered whether this artist, who lived and worked on unceded Musqueam, Squamish and Tsleil-Waututh territory, had any idea of the Squamish history of weaving. I wondered if he'd care that Squamish blankets were placed in an anthropology museum while his were given a solo exhibit in a respected art gallery.

Some things only matter when a white man does them.

Cynical and unimpressed, we left the gallery to wander towards Granville Island. We spent nearly an hour in a specialty stamp store. We tried terrible virtual reality, which made my eleven-year-old cry. We had fake ketchup sprayed at us by the owner of a magic shop, which annoyed me but made my husband and eleven-year-old absolutely giddy. We ate perogies and cake crafted to look like the Pride flag. It was, all in all, a pretty tame tourist experience. We only stopped at the Starbucks so we could use free Wi-Fi to map our trip back to our hotel room.

Then I saw the tweet. As I sat there reading the first article I could find, a lump lodged in my throat. Colten Boushie, who was a firekeeper, who would mow the lawns of elders in his community, whose friends were trying to get away from Gerald Stanley's farm shortly before Stanley's gun fired into the back of Boushie's head, would receive no justice. His family would know no peace.

As soon as the story of Boushie's death came to light, Gerald Stanley came to be considered something of a folk hero among white rural Canadians. He'd done what they all seemed willing — or even eager — to do: kill an Indian. Stanley's rationale — or lack thereof — didn't matter. The fact that Boushie was an important part of his community didn't matter. All that mattered was Stanley had killed an Indian, and like the Hollywood cowboys his actions emulated, he deserved not only his freedom but a bounty. Over the next few days, he'd get one. His GoFundMe page amassed over $100,000 within seventy-two hours.

Some things don't matter when a white man does them.

The first person to realize dark matter existed was Fritz Zwicky, an astronomer at the California Institute of Technology. In the 1930s, he was studying orbit patterns within the Coma Cluster, a cluster of over a thousand galaxies. Zwicky tried to calculate the mass of the cluster based on its velocity, which should have been straightforward using the virial theorem and Isaac Newton's theories on gravity. What he found, however, was that there was much more matter in the cluster than the light of its stars suggested. There was something unaccounted for that couldn't be seen. Zwicky called this mysterious, invisible force "dark matter."

The lump in my throat grew the entire bus ride home. I felt like I was going to vomit. I thought about Debbie Baptiste, who, upon hearing her son had died, screamed and collapsed to the ground. The Royal Canadian Mounted Police (RCMP), who were searching her house without her consent, asked if she was drunk. When you aren't seen as human, your human emotions are no longer relatable but indecipherable — evidence you're unstable or an animal or a drunk.

The injustice of Colten's death; the injustice of Colten's friends not only witnessing his murder but getting arrested; the injustice of Stanley drinking coffee with his family while Colten's body grew cold in their yard; the injustice of Debbie Baptiste's grief being read as drunkenness by RCMP officers tearing apart her house; the injustice of so many white Canadians referring to Colten as a criminal when Stanley was the one on trial for murder — it had all simmered inside for a year. And when I read that verdict and understood that, even in this era of so-called reconciliation, Canadians would continue to see Indigenous people as worthless criminals, and that pain finally, finally boiled over, I wanted to cry or scream or collapse. But I couldn't. I was in a Starbucks, then I was on a bus. Public pain was impolite. Someone could think I was drunk. Someone could call the cops. I kept myself composed, the way society expected me to; I tried to smile and laugh, the way society expected me to. My body was sharp glass I dutifully held together.

A few Indigenous friends told me later they couldn't sleep after the verdict. All I wanted to do was sleep. Plunge headfirst into a dreamscape where my family, friends and community weren't seen as disposable, where our deaths mattered, where our lives mattered. As long as I was dreaming, we could be respected and loved and seen as human.

I slept for nearly twelve hours that night.

In 1973, Princeton astronomers Jeremiah

Ostriker and James Peebles were studying how galaxies evolve. They built a computer simulation of a galaxy using a technique called N-body simulation. What they found, however, was that they couldn't recreate the elliptical or spiral shapes observable in most galaxies — until they added a uniform distribution of invisible mass. Suddenly, with the introduction of this dark matter, things reacted the way Ostriker and Peebles expected them to. Things started to make sense.

As Ostriker and Peebles were doing their simulations, astronomers Kent Ford and Vera Cooper Rubin were studying the motion of stars in the Andromeda galaxy at the Carnegie Institution of Washington. They measured the velocity of hydrogen gas clouds in and around the galaxy, expecting those outside the visible edge of the galaxy to be moving at a much slower rate than those on the edge. But the rate of velocity was the same.

For this to be the case, there had to be a considerable amount of dark matter both outside the edge of the Andromeda galaxy and within the galaxy itself. Rubin concluded that, despite dark matter's invisibility, it must be there — and in levels that increased the farther from the galactic centre one got. It would appear that dark matter was affecting the entire universe.

Aboriginal Peoples Television Network (APTN), a news organization that focuses on Indigenous issues, reported on a Facebook post by an unnamed RCMP officer regarding the Stanley verdict. "This should never have been allowed to be about race," the officer wrote. "Crimes were committed and a jury found the man not guilty in protecting his home and family. . . . Too bad the kid died but he got what he deserved."

Colten Boushie was sleeping when the SUV he was in pulled up to Gerald Stanley's farm. As far as we know from the testimony of both sides, he didn't try to steal anything. He never even left the vehicle. We would later learn his friends had attempted to break into another car earlier that day, after they realized theirs had a flat. But at the time, Stanley didn't know this. He saw them pull up, he heard Colten's friend get on an ATV and attempt to start it. This was all it took for Stanley's son to run at the SUV with a hammer and smash the windshield. Stanley himself kicked out the taillight before going to get his gun.

I have a feeling the Stanleys' actions were

not what the RCMP officer was referring to when he or she said "crimes were committed," though their damaging the SUV was, in fact, criminal and could be considered mischief under the Criminal Code of Canada. No, I have a feeling the officer was referring to the actions of Boushie's friends and their failed attempts at theft, despite the Criminal Code of Canada stating that theft is only completed once a person who intends to steal an item causes it to move. Since neither the car nor the ATV moved, theft did not occur. Still, the RCMP officer claims the violent, gun-toting Stanley was "protecting his home and family" and Colten "got what he deserved."

The first time I stole I was in fourth grade. My family had just moved to Painesville, Ohio, from the motel in Cleveland we'd been living in. Before that, we'd been living at a Salvation Army shelter in Buffalo, New York. You could say we were moving up in the world, though moving up from nothing doesn't require much.

There was a convenience store a few blocks from the mostly empty house we were renting. It sold twenty-five-cent Little Debbie pastries, which my sister, brother and I loved. My favourite were Fudge

Rounds — two chocolate cookies smashed together with chocolate cream in the middle, drizzled with fudge. My siblings loved Oatmeal Creme Pies, which were pretty much the same as Fudge Rounds except with oatmeal cookies and vanilla cream. I don't recall exactly when I decided we should steal them, but I knew that I wanted to make my siblings happy. I knew that we didn't have a lot of reasons to be happy. Little Debbie pastries seemed as good a reason as any.

If I bought something at the store, I reasoned, I'd be less suspicious. You can't be both a thief and a patron — or so I hoped the store clerks thought. My siblings and I would scan the streets for pennies, nickels and dimes, dig through couch cushions and crawl under car seats until we had twenty-five cents. Then we'd pull off the heist — taking far more pastries than we wanted when the clerk was looking, sticking a few in our pockets when she wasn't, then putting the rest back before settling on just one to buy.

The first few times it went well. Everyone in our neighbourhood looked poor; we fit in completely. When we moved to Mentor, Ohio, however — a much richer city — we were no longer just another poor mixed-race family in a community of poor mixed-race families; we were *the* poor mixed-race family in a white, middle-class community, living well outside our means.

The first time I tried to pull off a pastry heist there, I was caught. The clerk's eyes were on my sister and me as soon as we stepped in the door — taking in our stringy, uncut hair, our ill-fitting, donated clothes. She followed us around the store. She wasn't subtle about it. When my sister and I came to the cash register, the clerk said she knew we were stealing. She'd seen us pocketing treats in the reflection in the window. She looked at us with such disgust. She couldn't tell we were Indigenous, but she could tell we were incredibly poor.

The total cost of our attempted theft was no more than five dollars. Probably closer to three. It was almost nothing, but it was enough. We were no longer an eight- and ten-year-old under this woman's gaze; we were not sad kids trying to cope with poverty and abuse. We were thieves, criminals. Not-quite-humans who would one day get what we deserved.

But what did we deserve? To go to some juvenile detention facility and have our responses to poverty punished? How would her reaction have changed if we were visibly

Indigenous? Would she have called the cops then and there, as opposed to giving us the chance to leave and "wise up"? Did our white skin give us a chance at redemption my brown cousins wouldn't have gotten under the same circumstances?

When Stanley looked at Colten, did his face resemble that clerk's face when she looked at my sister and me? Was the same disgust curling his lip? The same sense of righteousness? Did he think of himself as some modern-day cowboy keeping the savage Indians at bay?

Unlike my sister and me, Colten didn't steal anything. So what did Colten, a twenty-two-year-old nêhiyaw man, deserve? To be killed after a day out with friends? To have the white man who fired the bullet that ultimately led to his death cleared of all legal and criminal responsibility for killing him? How is any of this "not about race"?

I suppose, in one sense, the RCMP officer is right. This should never have been allowed to be about race. Stanley and his son shouldn't have grown up in a society where Indians are portrayed as the biggest threat to life in the prairies, where cowboys killing Indians is viewed as heroic and worthy of hundreds of films, where the success of this country was dependent upon how close

Canada was to enacting "the final solution of our Indian Problem." Perhaps if those things hadn't been allowed to have been made about race, Colten and his friends might have felt comfortable asking white people like Stanley for help when they first got a flat tire, knowing that even though they'd been drinking, they'd still be seen as people who needed help and not just drunken Indians and potential threats. Or, if Colten and his friends were making reckless decisions — the types of decisions young people sometimes make, regardless of whether they're drinking or not — the punishment would be less severe and more humane than death by vigilante.

Maybe, if none of the history of Canada or Saskatchewan were allowed to be about race, Colten would still be here today.

According to NASA's website, despite over forty-five years of vigorous research since 1973, "We are much more certain what dark matter is not than we are what it is."

It is not in the form of stars or planets. It is not in the form of dark clouds or normal matter. It is not antimatter or black holes. It is not any of these things. It is always something else.

Perhaps we can't see dark matter because

we don't know what to look for. Perhaps we can't see it because we don't know how to look.

The next morning the lump in my throat was still there, and my family was still, technically, on vacation. We'd had plans for a full day in the city, ending with a trip to the HR MacMillan Space Centre and observatory. The Stanley verdict changed everything. I didn't have the energy to keep pretending I was a blissful tourist on unceded, stolen Indigenous land. I didn't have the privilege to forget what the Stanley verdict meant for my family, friends, community. I wanted to be around people who were mourning with me, who felt that deep, inescapable sorrow threatening to swallow us all.

My eleven-year-old was on the hotel room bed watching TV. I lay down next to them, took a deep breath, and explained the Stanley case, as every Indigenous parent no doubt did that morning. I told them that I was going to go to a rally to support justice for the Boushie family, that they didn't have to come if they didn't want to. "No, Mom, I want to come," they said. I nearly burst into tears, hugged them to my chest. I thanked genetics for giving them white skin to protect them from the racism that has killed both my visibly Indigenous grandfather and my visibly Indigenous uncle, felt sick that this was something I had to be thankful for. No one should have to feel thankful that their child isn't dark-skinned.

"We'll still go to the space centre later," I promised.

The vacation would go on, the way the rest of the world had.

My kid, my husband and I shivered in the cold outside the Canadian Broadcasting Company (CBC) Vancouver building.

It felt fitting that the rally started there. A year and a half earlier, just three days after Colten's death, CBC Saskatoon chose to publish an editorial on Canadians' right to defend property, carelessly framing Colten's death as potentially justifiable before any information was really known about the case. CBC Ombudsman Esther Enkin even defended this article, claiming that since the RCMP hadn't immediately laid charges against Stanley, and three of Colten's friends had been taken into custody for potential "property-related offences," the self-defence argument was part of public discourse. Apparently CBC had a responsibility to the public to offer "diverse perspectives" — though Enkin did admit that a line in the article that implied self-defence would form the backbone of the criminal proceedings was unclear and misleading.

By now, we know that Stanley's lawyer knew better than to claim the fifty-four-year-old was defending himself against a group of teenagers trying to drive away from him and his hammer-wielding son on a flat tire; that a just-woken twenty-two-year-old posed any significant threat to a man trying to commandeer their vehicle while holding a gun. By now we also know that Stanley's lawyer never had to make that argument in the courtroom. Others were already making it for him. It materialized on social media, in Facebook posts and online comments made largely by white Canadians. It materialized in a resolution to call for the federal government to expand self-defence laws in Canada, passed by 92 percent of the Saskatchewan Association of Rural Municipalities less than a month after Colten's death. It materialized in my Twitter mentions when I posted anger and pain at the injustice of Stanley's acquittal. It was everywhere, all the time. In that sense, I suppose we could have started the rally outside nearly any building in Canada and it would have had

96

the same symbolic effect.

Over three hundred people turned out that day. Speaker after speaker came to the front of the crowd, ranging from the Skatin and Sts'ailes dancer and missing and murdered Indigenous women advocate Lorelei Williams, to Stō:lo/St'át'imc/ Nlaka' pamux multi media artist and hip hop musician Ronnie Dean Harris, to Sapotaweyak Cree Nation slam poetry champion and artist jaye simpson. Some people were passing out traditional medicines to the crowd. Some were handing out red ribbons for people to wrap around their arms in solidarity. Some were taking around smudge, filling the air with the warm, comforting scent of sage. Some carried photos of Colten they'd printed out before coming.

Even though I was only standing in a crowd, even though I was only marching through Vancouver streets, even though I was only lighting candles on the steps of the courthouse where we eventually stopped, it felt good to be doing something with my body. It felt good to think there was a plan others had laid out for me, and all I had to do was follow it. It felt good that there was a place to hold my pain, my child's pain, that other Indigenous people had made this space for us.

97

"When I say 'Justice,' you say 'For Colten,' " Nuxalk and Onondaga hip hop artist JB The First Lady called to us.

"Justice!"

"For Colten!"

"Justice!"

"For Colten!"

My kid, my husband and I yelled until we were hoarse. Our voices, it seemed, were all we could give — that, and ten dollars towards speaker rentals.

It's strange to think that most of the matter in the universe is invisible. We know dark matter exists, we see its effects, but we cannot point to it and say, "There it is! That's dark matter! Look at it! I told you it existed!"

Maybe our single-minded focus on the light makes us unable to see the dark that's all around, always. Like when you turn off the lights in a bright room and, for the first few seconds, you can't make out shapes you saw so clearly moments before. In those first few seconds of dark, your eyes would have you believe there's nothing else there. But your eyes are wrong. Something is there, whether you see it or not.

The first recorded use of the word "racism"

was in 1902. The man who used it was an American named Richard Henry Pratt. He was criticizing racial segregation, arguing that it "[killed] the progress of the segregated people" and that all classes and races should come together to "destroy racism and classism."

But, as writer Gene Demby points out, "Although Pratt might have been the first person to inveigh against racism and its deleterious effects by name, he is much better-remembered for a very different coinage: Kill the Indian . . . save the man."

Pratt was what might be called a benevolent racist. Unlike his more extreme contemporaries, Pratt believed that there was no need to kill all Indians, that the problem was not Indians themselves but "all the Indian there is in the race." In other words, he wanted the same thing that Canada has wanted for centuries: assimilation. He even advocated for Indian boarding schools, the United States' version of residential schools, ultimately creating the infamous Carlisle Indian Industrial School out of an abandoned military post. Indigenous children were taken from their homes and forced to speak English, wear Western clothing, cut their hair, forsake their ceremonies and traditions. They were told to be ashamed of being Indigenous, to be ashamed of their own families. Many could not communicate with their parents when they went home, if they went home at all. Many were abused. Many were malnourished. Many got sick. Many died.

These stories filter through our families, told in actions more than words — each former student now raising their own kids the way their boarding school teachers had raised them. A legacy of shame and violence, trauma and pain, passed on from generation to generation like so many secrets.

And this from the mind of a man who spoke out against segregation and racism.

If Pratt had lived to see the impact of his life's work, I wonder if he would feel remorse. If he would see that what he did to Indigenous families was another form of the segregation and racism he claimed to denounce. I wonder if, upon hearing the Truth and Reconciliation Commission of Canada refer to residential schools as "cultural genocide," he'd realize that he was responsible for that exact thing in America, and apologize until his vocal cords stopped working.

More than likely, though, he'd just tell us we had it coming. That what he did wasn't racist at all, and we shouldn't be allowed to make any of this about race.

When we finally got to the HR MacMillan Space Centre, the sky was too cloudy to see any stars at the observatory. Instead my husband, my kid and I decided to head into the planetarium to watch a film called "Phantom of the Universe: The Search for Dark Matter." We leaned back and stared at a giant dome screen as Tilda Swinton explained the origins of the universe to us.

Dark matter forms the skeleton of our universe.

Dark matter doesn't emit light or reflect it. That's why scientists can't detect it.

The dark matter particle doesn't let anything stand in its way.

I wondered how something could be so pervasive, so all-en-compassing, responsible for the world as we know it, and still not be able to be clearly seen.

Then I remembered what Gerald Stanley's lawyer said about Colten's murder in his closing argument: "It's a tragedy, but it's not criminal." I remembered the Saskatchewan Association of Rural Municipalities trying to push for stronger self-protection laws while simultaneously denying the influence the Boushie murder had had on this deci-

101

sion. I remembered the white people on Twitter flooding Indigenous people's accounts with racist slurs; claims that Stanley was acting in self-defence; claims that Colten was a criminal who had it coming; that Stanley's white lawyer dismissing all visibly Indigenous people from the jury as soon as he saw them was not racist; that an all-white jury finding Stanley innocent of any wrongdoing when he shot Colten point-blank in the head was not racist; that none of this was racist. I remembered all the times I've pointed out racism in my life and the white people around me claimed I was imagining it. I remembered that, eventually, I started to wonder if I really was imagining it. I am always made to feel as if I am imagining it.

To these people, the only words, actions or thoughts that can be considered real racism are those they can't be blamed for. Could any one of them point to an instance of racism they'd witnessed today? This week? This month? Could they listen to you describe one you've witnessed and not stare blankly until you doubted your own perceptions, your own sanity?

I'm writing this less than a week after yet another unjust verdict. Raymond Cormier was the fifty-six-year-old white man accused of murdering Tina Fontaine, a fifteen-year-old Anishinaabe girl from Sagkeeng First Nation. Tina's seventy-two-pound body was found in Winnipeg's Red River, weighted down with rocks and wrapped in a comforter that witnesses claim Cormier owned. After decades of grassroots work by Indigenous women and family members went unrecognized, Tina's death finally brought the issue of missing and murdered Indigenous women, girls and two-spirited people into Canada's national consciousness. This is racism, Canada finally seemed able to say. This is wrong.

Then came the trial. In recordings, Cormier talked about how he had sex with Tina, how he was furious that she was only fifteen, how he was worried he'd be imprisoned if the cops found out he'd slept with her. He was seen fighting with Tina after he sold her bike for drug money. She threatened to call the cops on him for stealing a truck. In the recordings, Cormier seems to admit that he killed her. Still, he was found innocent. His lawyer didn't even have to offer a defence. He called no witnesses, offered no evidence. I suppose he didn't have to. The evidence washed away in the river.

Police officers, emergency workers and

social workers saw Tina the day she died. When police pulled over the truck she was in, they ran her name and saw that she was the subject of a missing person report, but they didn't help her. They left her there. When she was found hours later sleeping between cars in a parking lot, paramedics took her to the hospital. The doctor expressed concern that Tina was being sexually exploited, reportedly urging Tina not to run away from Child and Family Services, but still discharged her. From there, Tina's social worker took her to eat some McDonald's and set her up at a new hotel room. She encouraged Tina to stay on the premises, but later said there was no way to stop her from leaving if she wanted to. Then she drove away. Tina's great-aunt Thelma Favel wasn't informed any of the four times her niece went missing while in CFS's custody. When Favel called on August 15 to check on Tina, her social worker said she'd been missing for two weeks. The woman had apparently forgotten to tell Favel. Two days later Tina, who once wanted to grow up to be a CFS worker, was found dead. But none of this is evidence of racism, I suppose. It never is.

When I heard the Cormier verdict, my family was back in Brantford. I was alone in a residence room waiting for the verdict to be announced. As soon as my phone started buzzing, I knew what had happened. What had happened again, and will no doubt happen again and again and again and again to Indigenous people in this country and every country.

Three years after Tina's body was pulled from the Red River in Canada, another Indigenous woman was found in the same river on the other side of the medicine line that divides the U.S. and Canada. Savanna LaFontaine-Greywind, a 22-year-old woman from Spirit Lake Sioux First Nation, was found dead in North Dakota, her body duct-taped inside a garbage bag. She had been eight months pregnant when her neighbour, a white woman named Brooke Crews, offered her $20 to model a dress she claimed to be sewing. Savanna took care of elders for a living, and had recently put a down payment on an apartment so she could move in with her longtime boyfriend, Ashton Matheny, once their baby was born.

Shortly after entering her neighbor's apartment, Savanna was attacked by Crews who cut her unborn baby from her body. Crews' boyfriend, a white man named William Hoehn, helped Crews cover up Savanna's murder. When police came to search the apartment, Hoehn lied and told them that Savanna's parents, the Greywinds, were terrorists, that they smoked meth. Meanwhile, Hoehn himself was stoned, drinking a beer and playing video games, Savanna's newborn baby hidden in blankets right beside him. Savanna's body was inside a cubby hole in the bathroom, where it remained through a second police search, and might have remained for the next two searches, as well, had the couple not had ample opportunity to dump Savanna in the Red River.

Unlike Stanley and Cormier, Crews and Hoehn were both convicted for their crimes in 2018. They were given decades-long prison sentences. Yet, after the initial relief of seeing them convicted faded, I was left feeling hollow. While I hoped these convictions gave some peace to Savanna's family, I knew they wouldn't wash away centuries of systemic racism. They couldn't. That wasn't what the criminal justice system was designed for.

Are these guilty verdicts really justice? I still mourn for Savanna. I mourn for her surviving child, Haisley Jo. I mourn for her parents, who loved her desperately. I mourn for her partner, who must now raise their daughter alone. I mourn for the Red River, which has been turned into a graveyard, forced to hold Savanna, Tina and so many other Indigenous people in its depths, waiting for their kin to find them.

I don't know what justice is, but I know it's not this.

Racism, for many people, seems to occupy space in very much the same way as dark matter: it forms the skeleton of our world, yet remains ultimately invisible, undetectable. This is convenient. If nothing is racism, then nothing needs to be done to address it. We can continue on as usual. Answer emails. Teach classes. Go to dinner with our families. Go to space centres. Continue our vacations, untroubled. We can keep our eyes shut inside this dark room we've created and pretend that, as long as we can't see what's around us, there's nothing around us at all. After all, there's no proof of it. If the man who coined the term "racism" can despise everything that makes me Indian and get away with it, why the hell can't you?

SCRATCH

Most people's memories of their childhood are lush with sensory details: your mother's thick, slightly sweet spaghetti sauce; your grandfather's persistent smell of tobacco and oranges; the tiny "hmph" your sister made whenever one of her elaborate lies was unravelled. For me, there is one consistent detail and, unfortunately, it's far from romantic: my childhood itches. This makes sense, since I had head lice for over a decade. My relationship with head lice was, until recently, the longest relationship I'd ever had. Since the age of eight my fingernails were constantly scraping against my scalp, my hands always feeling, unseeing, for tiny eggs like seed beads strung on the strands of my thick, frizzy hair. Through state lines, too-small rental properties, homeless shelters and motel rooms, all the way to a trailer on the Six Nations reserve, those bugs nestled in the nape of my neck were the one constant in my life. I hated them but, in a way, I almost empathized with them. As a poor, mixed-race kid, I was treated like a parasite, too. I was unnecessary, unwanted, a social bloodsucker. I needed to be eradicated.

I first caught head lice at my grandparents' sprawling property on the rez. We were there visiting for the powwow. A ridiculous number of relatives came; tents popped up on the front lawn like dandelions. Though my cousins came down every summer, it was my first time being there. Needless to say, I felt a bit out of place. My mother did nothing to ease my fears, muttering about how my siblings and I were being treated differently because we were half-white. I had numerous cousins who were half-white, so I'm not sure how she justified this, but it added to my eight-year-old sense of loneliness nonetheless.

The first night, our parents drank beer and played radio bingo — or most of our parents. My mother was devoutly sober, a trait that further isolated her from her in-laws. The kids, meanwhile, were everywhere: hanging from the tire swing in the front yard, throwing brush into a bonfire precariously situated on the side of a hill, catching crayfish and catfish in the meagre depths of the creek. My six-year-old sister Missy and I took up with my fiery, hilarious six-year-old cousin Melita. She was basically the only one who acknowledged our existence. All our other cousins were already part of well-established family cliques, so familiar with one another it was like they were speaking their own language. We spent all our time together: playing hide and go seek, pulling wood ticks off one another's legs, running from stray rez dogs. When Melita asked if she could sleep in our tent that night, it was a revelation of sorts. *You are wanted. You belong.*

The next day we all started scratching.

That fall, after much pushing and persuasion, Mom finally got what she had been asking for for years: a proper Catholic upbringing for her children. Dad agreed to let my sister and me leave Native American Magnet School #19 — the only school in the city we could learn our culture — and enroll in a private Catholic school, which would be paid for with the help of my grandmother.

I became *the new kid,* a designation I'd wear like a runner-up sash for the next ten years. At Magnet School #19 my sister and

I managed to fly under the radar because the poverty was widespread; there were levels. As long as there were kids poorer and more socially awkward than us, we were safe. At this school, in this two-floored, wide-lawned part of town, it was just us. Luckily we wore uniforms, so it was hard to tell exactly how dirt poor we were. I tried to make myself so likeable that economics didn't matter, making jokes and faking a crush on John, the fourth-grader all the girls in my class obsessively pined after. He reminded me of a prepubescent Pat Sajak and had the personality of a broom handle, but I was so desperate to be accepted I didn't care. I hastily replaced my surname with his and scribbled it everywhere — my folders, my desk, my arms. The Catholic schoolgirls were impressed.

That victory was tempered by an even bigger defeat. While my parents made intermittent payments for my private schooling, they didn't pay rent on our house, so within a few months we were homeless. At that time my family included my mother and father, myself, Missy, my older half-sister Teena and my two-year-old brother Jon. The six of us squeezed into spare beds at my maternal grandmother's house. It was large, with six bedrooms and two bathrooms, but she was the caretaker of three elderly people, so most of the rooms were already spoken for. It was hardly ideal sharing a bedroom with my sister, grandmother and parents, but at least I didn't feel like an outsider. My mother told us Burgard Place was a "nice" neighbourhood when she was growing up, which meant it was mostly white. By the time my family and I moved in, it was mostly low-income Black families that lived there, the vibrant sixties paint having faded to light yellows and dull greens. I had no problem making friends with the neighbourhood kids. They didn't judge me for being poor or having parents that yelled at each other constantly; they were in the same position. We bonded over our love of Jonathan Taylor Thomas and TLC, shared our sorrow over the spells in *The Craft* being too demanding to actually perform (who has access to all those animals and candles?) and Tupac's untimely death.

By that point we'd had unnoticed and untreated head lice for months. We were positively crawling with them. The only way my parents figured it out was through my grandmother, who noticed one of the women she cared for scratching incessantly. Hundreds of dollars of Nix bottles were placed on the counter. Everyone's hair was treated, everyone's sheets were washed. I remember my grandmother's face as she applied the prescription shampoo to my head: her lips tight, downturned, the perfect blend of annoyance and disgust. I'd seen her look at other people with that face — the people she cared for, my parents, the parish priest on occasion. She'd never looked at me like that, though. Not before that night.

Then my uncle Jerry came crashing into the picture. Uncle Jerry was a heroin addict. With gaunt cheeks and a big, bushy beard, he resembled Jesus on the shroud of Turin, only Uncle Jerry wore a David Foster Wallace–style bandana and the same plaid button-up shirt every day. He was homeless, too, so my grandmother gathered him in and gave him the basement — the same place my family was temporarily storing nearly all of our things. Within weeks, my dad's expensive stereo system went missing. He blamed my uncle, saying he'd sold it for drug money. My grandma offered no evidence to counter this, no apology or shame on her son's behalf. She simply told my dad to drop it. My dad was working at Sun Television and Appliances at the time and had won that stereo system in a sales competition. It was a trophy for him, recognition, a small sign that he'd accomplished something when his current circumstances were telling him the exact opposite. He wasn't going to drop anything. He was going to stew, collect grievances and spit them in Mom's ear, poisoning her against her own family. Then he was going to wait for the inevitable.

Like any good Catholic woman, my mother modelled herself after the Virgin Mary. She prayed the rosary every day, regularly visited the Dominican nunnery, made us watch the Catholic channel EWTN for hours in what felt like *Clockwork Orange*–style sessions. Her religious devotion was inconvenient when I wanted to watch cartoons, but I still admired it, viewing her with a reverence bordering on holiness. She'd regularly tell me about her labour with me: how she was hooked up to a myriad of IVs and monitoring devices for eighteen hours before I was finally born. She was so dedicated to being my mother she nearly died. I'm sure she didn't mean for this story to chronicle, even mythologize, her love for me, but it did. As far as I was concerned, the Virgin Mary had nothing on her.

This is what made her sudden transition so jarring. Once Uncle Jerry started causing problems, my mom would snap at me for small things. Her eyes would focus, unblinking, her face would harden, her lips so chapped they resembled desert mud cracks. I didn't notice the change in her at first because, at that point, all the adults in my life were constantly angry. I never knew what would set them off. It was like I was walking a perpetual tightrope. Sooner or later I'd have to fall.

It finally erupted one day in September. My uncle was carrying around a white bucket of hot tar, stirring it with a smooth piece of wood. He planned to use it on my grandmother's driveway. At the same time he was arguing with my mother. His eyes were wide and blue, angry like my mom's. Then he tried to fling hot tar at her. His aim was off; instead of my mother, it hit my two-year-old brother Jon in the face. There was screaming and crying and more chaos than I'd ever witnessed. The scariest part was no one was taking control of the situation. Things didn't stop when my brother was hurt; they intensified. My mother cradled Jon with one hand while she tensed the other, darting a steely finger into my uncle's chest, accusing. My uncle stood before her, aflame with anger.

No one was acting like an adult. Or rather, they weren't acting like the responsible adults I saw calmly reasoning their way through family squabbles on *The Fresh Prince of Bel-Air.* They weren't sturdy and dependable like Uncle Phil and Aunt Viv; they were much worse — emotional, fallible, human. My father wasn't there. My grandmother wasn't there. My older sister wasn't there. At eight years old, I found myself the only person in the house who wanted to act responsibly, so I did the one thing eight-year-olds are told to do when things get bad: I dialed 911.

Turns out that was a bad idea. My parents were angry at me for bringing the police into matters. My grandmother was livid. That all seemed backwards to me. I thought the big deal was my brother being burned, unintentionally or not. Instead I was being lectured on "family business staying private." I don't know if my grandmother knew that my uncle had burned my brother. There's a scar on Jon's face to this day so she wouldn't have had to look hard for evidence. I do know she told my parents we had to get out of her house immediately — and we had to leave Teena with her. I couldn't understand why Teena was the chosen one. I wondered if it was because she had blonde hair and blue eyes. She was completely white, not just half, like me. We

116

packed what we could and, minus Teena, settled into a room at the closest Salvation Army, homeless again.

Without my grandmother's financial aid, payments towards my private schooling fell behind. I was still driven to school every day, still allowed to sit in my normal seat in class, but even that started to feel precarious, as if the Jenga tower of our lives was one sharp tug from tumbling.

Then it did.

One evening my mom came to pick up Missy and me from the after-school program. As soon as she stepped in the room, words were pouring from her mouth — a swirling, manic saga mixing our real-life family drama with sections of the Bible and *The Catholic Catechism,* complete with references to demons and witchcraft. She wasn't speaking to anyone in particular. Her story required no audience. It was as if her words were summoning her into existence, making her real, and if she paused for even the space of a breath she'd disappear. The rants were a lifeline, a plea. *Help. Someone help.*

The teachers reacted with judgment and disgust. They asked if she, a sober woman with an addict for a brother, was on drugs.

When this made her even more upset, they asked her to leave. She was scaring the other kids.

After that Child and Family Services began circling our fragmented family. In hindsight, I'm surprised we managed to avoid their attention for as long as we did. My father tried to contain things. He quickly had my mother hospitalized while we were at school one day, then warned me a social worker was coming to talk to me. He said it was very important that I make her think everything was fine, that I was happy. If I didn't, she could decide to take us away and break our family even more. I don't remember what I said to the social worker but it must have been good enough. We weren't dragged away screaming. We were still at the Salvation Army with my dad, waiting, surviving.

Almost as soon as my mom was released from the hospital, my father declared we were moving to Ohio. My mom had family in Euclid we'd met exactly once. Her father had gone to art school in Cleveland. Apart from that, Ohio meant nothing to any of us. I'm not sure what my dad thought he was running to. I don't think he did, either. All that mattered was that he was running.

Before he met my mom he'd spent his entire life running — from jobs, relationships, from his traditional territory. Any time he took a step forward, one foot was always stubborn and still, waiting for him to turn and bolt. To him, running was easy. Running was safe. And the possibility of reinvention, of abandoning whatever mess he'd made and starting fresh, was always too tempting to resist.

When you have a wife and kids, though, it's much harder to do that. We holed up in a motel room while my father looked for a job and a place for us to live. After a year of bouncing between empty, echoing rental houses and motel rooms, we settled in Mentor, Ohio. My dad took up selling satellite services door to door. My mom's time was split between home and various mental health units, a grim carousel that never stopped.

What also didn't stop was my father's libido. Once again Mom got pregnant, which would bring our family's head count back to six. As angry as my parents were with my grandma, especially after she fought for, and won, full custody of Teena, they still needed the money she was willing to provide. Battle-axes were dropped and a tentative normalcy resumed. My parents even let Grandma take all of us kids for the summer so Mom would be able to care for the new baby, Mikey, in relative peace. Grandma and Teena spoiled us with gifts, trips to restaurants and amusement parks, luxuries our parents could rarely provide at home. We were all happy that things were finally okay — until Teena saw a louse scurrying through my hair while we were at church. She dragged us home and treated our hair, black garbage bags tied over her hands like absurd inflatable mittens. When my grandma came home and heard how we'd spent our afternoon, she decided we couldn't come to her house again unless we were lice-free. She was the one stable adult in my life, and she had cast me out. I was devastated. It felt like she was punishing us for something we couldn't control.

I'd never trust her again.

Every time Mom came home an hourglass was turned, and we had only so much time before she was back in the mental health ward again. My dad was very careful about it, only ever having her hospitalized while we were at school. We'd come home and he'd be there instead of her, explaining to us what we'd already guessed.

One day Missy, Jon and I got off the bus

to find Mom had set up my brother Mikey in his high chair on the front lawn. She was pacing and yelling about God and my father and the Devil, her face red, her eyes wide with rage. We hoped none of the kids on the bus could see her acting weird, but apart from that we weren't really worried. This sometimes happened to Mom. Which is probably why we were all so surprised when a police officer knocked on our door. A neighbour had called the cops. Mom pooled her considerable intellectual resources to convince the officer he was wasting his time. She was feeding her child on the lawn because it was a nice day. Was there some law against that? Her logic was surprisingly sturdy, even in the throes of illness. At that point, her diagnosis had gone from schizophrenia to postpartum depression to manic depression. Some people, like my grandmother and Teena, were convinced there was nothing wrong with her at all. It really depended on who she was speaking with and how "on" she was.

Still, she couldn't fool my dad. She didn't even try. As soon as he got home from hours of white suburban doors slamming in his wide Mohawk face, she'd start in, recounting their unsavoury history in grotesque detail, making horrific accusations, her face inches from his as she trailed him from room to room. It was as if she needed to make him pay for her pain. Dad usually started off quiet, but eventually he erupted, too, calling her crazy, threatening that no judge would ever give her custody of us. Neither of them seemed to care that we could hear every word. Out of politeness we tried to pretend we were in a parallel dimension, just watching Nickelodeon on the couch while the next universe over they screamed and cried.

The last grain of sand in her hourglass fell again. She was gone by the time we came home the next day.

After three years I'd forgotten what it was like to *not* itch my head every five minutes. Through experience I had taught myself covert ways to scratch the lice so as not to bring attention to them. I scratched while flipping my hair, or running my fingers through it, or while leaning my head on my hand in a perfect imitation of preteen boredom. I even trained myself to keep from scratching as long as possible, hoping my steely determination would force the tiny bugs to wave a white flag and leave my scalp, defeated.

Despite my attempts to appear lice-free,

the staff at Dale R. Rice Elementary would not be fooled. They had random head lice checks. One thing I'll say about this particular upper-middle-class school is that they had considerable tact. I wasn't singled out when the nurse found a small country of bugs in my hair. They called me down to the office over the intercom once everyone was back in class, claiming I had "an appointment," mercifully omitting that appointment was with a bottle of medicated shampoo and a fine-tooth comb.

With my mother in the hospital, my dad had to deal with this round alone. He opted to totally shave off Jon's hair. Jon wasn't impressed. In his first grade school photo he looks like he missed Christmas. Dad treated my sister and me, but given his track record we had very little faith in his abilities. Being independent young women of nine and eleven, we decided to deal with it ourselves. Every night we'd close the door to our bedroom, turn on the TV and start picking nits out of each other's hair. To us, this seemed like a foolproof plan. We would not only be allowed back at Grandma's house, we'd also help out our hapless parents.

Eventually I figured out there was a fundamental flaw in our plan: we pulled the nits from one another's hair and deposited them directly onto our carpeted floor, where they'd hatch and climb onto our beds, couches and clothes. So our objective changed. Instead of getting rid of the lice — which was clearly impossible — we would focus on getting rid of the really obvious bright white nits, hoping the hard-to-spot dark brown ones we left behind would go undetected by the head lice squad at school. It wasn't the worst plan. After all, that was the way every type of social service seemed to approach our unsavoury realities: don't solve the problems of poverty or racism or violence or mental illness. Just hide them away.

It actually worked for a while. No one could tell there was an entire ecosystem on our heads, and since no one could tell, no one cared. This was helped along immensely by my entry into junior high the next year. The school was so big no one dared recommend a school-wide lice check. Olly olly oxen free.

Child and Family Services continued to pop in regularly. My father prepped us like key witnesses in a murder trial: readymade answers to probable questions, a list of dos and don'ts. Do mention everything is fine.

Don't mention Mom and Dad's raging fights or the head lice.

We didn't have any problem shaking them off. The stakes were too high. We knew none of those social workers were interested in repairing our broken family. They were waiting for the right time to take a sledgehammer to it, scatter the shards and call it a job well done. Regardless of our parents' feelings for one another, which were becoming more and more toxic, I knew that none of us kids were in their crosshairs, at least not overtly. Instead of targeting us for violence, our parents would turn our sympathy into weapons to use against each other. If we witnessed anything, either physical or verbal, we would immediately come to the defence of the person being attacked. Mom didn't utilize this as dramatically as Dad did — he would make a show of the slightest shove — but Mom still had much more historical material to draw from, considering how long and how badly Dad had abused her. The constant manipulation was like getting hit with shrapnel: painful enough, but nowhere near as bad as direct hits. As the oldest child, I took on the responsibility of refereeing their fights, sending the youngest siblings into another room to watch TV while I picked a side and screamed my allegiance. I could handle them, I told myself. My siblings were safe as long as I was around. I needed to be able to see them, to protect them from the stress of managing two warring adults. I couldn't do that in a foster home.

Against all odds, my parents had another son, Dakota. Now there were seven of us squeezing into a three-bedroom house in Mentor. The space was too tight, the neighbours were too close. The police continued to be called on us whenever my mom was ill, my mother continued her biannual residency at the hospital. My father was looking for an out, I could feel it. We all were.

As if on cue, my dad's stepfather died back in Canada. While my grandparents' beautiful house was left to my aunt, a considerable patch of land behind it was Dad's for the taking. Within a week of hearing the news, Dad was done with Mentor, done with Ohio, done with the United States of America. He was heading out to find gold and glory on a new frontier: the Six Nations reserve.

Right before we moved, Missy and I borrowed a Ouija board from one of my friends. We knew our mother wouldn't approve, so we used it out in the woods behind our house. We asked the usual teenage girl questions about boys and boobs. Then my sister asked one I wasn't expecting: "How old will I be when we get rid of the lice?" The planchette sat unmoving for a moment, then gradually moved to the numbers 1 and 6. Five years away. That meant I'd be eighteen.

I remembered my grandparents' house on Six Nations as the pinnacle of luxury and beauty. Cupboards stocked with cookies and unopened products from the Home Shopping Network. Hundreds of channels playing on tons of TVs. Dolls dressed up like Indian girls I'd never resemble. And surrounding everything, most magical of all, planters. Hanging white planters and large plastic planters and small terracotta planters spilling out snapdragons and pansies and tulips.

We, on the other hand, moved into a two-bedroom trailer with fake wood panelling and no running water. Our electricity came from an exceedingly complicated network of extension cords, strung up and spliced to shit by my father. Our heat came from a tiny wood-burning stove in the living room. For the first few months we paid for a port-a-potty to be set up next to the trailer. Eventually that became too expensive, so we used a commode that we dumped in the woods whenever the bucket got too full. To wash meant pouring water from a giant blue jug into a pot, heating it on the stove, then sponging ourselves off in the otherwise useless bathroom. Washing our hair was the same, though we did that over the kitchen sink once we removed all the dishes, still sticky with ketchup and leftover Kraft Dinner.

Dad told us that he'd have running water and full electricity within a year.

Missy and I had stopped nit-picking one another, but any time one of my younger brothers had the misfortune of laying his head on my lap, my fingers would instinctively start sifting through his hair. It was easy enough to find the white nits in nearly black strands, but I prided myself on being able to find the incognito eggs so many school nurses had overlooked. I'd also started compulsively nit-picking myself. I'd slide my hand through my hair until I felt them like tiny poppy seeds scattered at my scalp, grasp them between two fingers, then dig the nail of my index finger into the flesh of my thumb and pull to the ends of my hair. I'd do it for hours, unthinking, until there were indentations in my thumbs. I didn't bother to hide what I was doing. I knew I was crossing some invisible, unspoken line; like my mother's mental illness, we did not speak of the lice unless we absolutely had to. Still, I was desperate for normalcy. This seemed like the only thing I could control, the only thing I had any chance to change. I had to get rid of the lice.

Yet despite my best intentions, I couldn't change the facts. To really treat lice, you need to treat everyone at the same time, wash any clothes that may have been contaminated, wash any sheets that have been contaminated, vacuum floors and couches and mattresses, then do it all again in seven to ten days to prevent reinfestation. We were five kids and two adults with barely enough money to pay for our normal loads at the laundromat. Plus, even after a year, even after two years, even after five years, we still had no running water. Those were the facts. What's more, we were tired. My dad still treated us with Nix and spent hours combing our hair with a fine-tooth comb whenever any of us were sent home from school, but I could see he'd given up. Lice were inescapable, part of the package.

My mother's mental illness kept coming back like a nightmarish refrain. She'd be gone once, twice, three times a year, leaving me to mother my siblings, make some din-

ners, wash some clothes. Though our neighbours were now too far away to either hear
my parents screaming or see Mom doing
anything they might deem worth a 911 call,
that didn't keep the social workers at bay.
Two of my siblings went to one school, and
two went to another, a Mohawk immersion
school. There were frequent head lice
checks at both. My youngest brothers got
sent home every single time. Eventually
their school notified the Children's Aid
Society. As soon as we found out we
scrubbed everything. The trailer was never
as clean as it was before social workers were
scheduled to show. Like a stage director,
Dad would block the scene. He made sure
the living room and kitchen looked nice,
that we were all sitting obediently on the
couch, that we had our scripts memorized,
then gently encouraged the social worker to
interview each of us outside. That way she
couldn't see how cramped the two bedrooms were or witness the horror that was
our bathroom. It worked. It always did.

It used to strike me as strange the way
social workers and police officers flocked to
our family. My siblings and I were great
students. We had no problems at school; no
mysterious bruises discoloured our skin. We
were liked by our teachers, made friends

easily. Any time any of us played sports, our dad was in the stands and in the coach's ear, politicking our way to better positions. Our mom knew the names of all of our friends, even though we were too embarrassed to invite them to meet her. We never went hungry. We never lacked for love or encouragement. Our parents were far from perfect, but their main barriers to being better parents were poverty, intergenerational trauma and mental illness — things neither social workers nor police officers have ever been equipped to address, yet are both allowed, even encouraged, to patrol.

Of course I know now it's not strange at all that our family was monitored by child services. Indigenous kids in Canada are anywhere from five to twelve times more likely to be taken into government care than non-Indigenous kids, depending on province. In the U.S. that stat is much lower thanks to the 1978 Indian Child Welfare Act; as of 2019, Native kids are 2.7 times more likely to be taken into care than the national average. While this is still very much a problem, it's far better than the reality Native families faced before 1978. Back then, 25-35 percent of all Native children in the country were being separated from their families and put into foster care.

The main reason cited for taking Native kids away from their parents is neglect. Nico Trocmé, Director of McGill University's School of Social Work, says that, in these cases, "neglect" is another word for poverty. In an interview with *The Tyee,* he says, "I've certainly never seen any evidence from any of the research to indicate that there is something endemic to First Nations families that would explain a higher rate of placement. It has much more to do with the high rates of poverty and the difficult social and economic circumstances they're living in." In other words, social services conflates not being able to afford adequate housing, food, clothing and health care with *choosing* not to have adequate housing, food, clothing and health care. Instead of supporting poor families and helping them become financially secure, social services' approach is to simply take the kids. It's as though they believe that removing the added expenses of children is doing poor parents a favour, or taking kids from loving parents and throwing them in impersonal, sometimes dangerous foster homes is doing *them* a favour. As anyone who has had experience with child welfare might anticipate, the effects of this policy are disastrous. Every year, approximately 20,000 of the youth in foster care in the United States age out of the system, often without positive supports or family connections to help them with the adjustment. Within 18 months of aging out, 40-50 percent of those youth become homeless. Add to that the fact that former foster youth are more likely to have poor physical and mental health outcomes; more likely to abuse drugs and alcohol; more likely to experience unplanned pregnancies; and more likely to deal with unemployment, and you should have a pretty good idea of how effective our current child welfare system is when it comes to protecting vulnerable youth.

It would seem, then, that Indigenous children have more reason to fear governmental care than they do their parents' poverty. In some sense I intuited this, even as a kid. I knew it was bullshit that social workers and cops had so much control over our family, that they could split us up the moment we didn't cater to their sensibilities. Knowing this then made me hate social workers and cops. Knowing this now makes me hate the systems that empower them — systems that put families in impossible situations, then punish them for not being able to claw their way out.

■ ■ ■ ■

Though we never met her strict no-lice requirement, my grandmother eventually lifted my family's banishment from her house. Still, ever since that first expulsion, I had a strong fear of spreading my lice to others. If I ever slept anywhere that wasn't my house, I insisted on wearing a sweatshirt to bed, pulling the hood up over my ponytail before I laid my head down. It wasn't a great method of containment. At seventeen I spread lice to my high school boyfriend. He was sure he'd caught them from sleeping outside on a camping trip, but when he jokingly suggested that he probably caught them from me, I felt sick. I knew he did. He got rid of them easily enough, but as long as he was with me he would never be safe. His life would become mine: always scratching, always feeling like a contaminant.

I tried to break up with him that day. When he asked why, I couldn't give him the real reason, and I couldn't give a fake one with any amount of conviction, so I reluctantly gave in and stayed, promising myself I'd be more vigilant. Promising myself if he caught it one more time, I'd leave.

Within six months I was pregnant.

■ ■ ■ ■

I finally got rid of my head lice at eighteen. I could only do it by leaving my parents' house. Part of me always knew that. With only one head to treat, access to running water, enough spare cash to pay for two rounds of medication and all the necessary laundry, delousing myself was considerably easier than I'd thought it'd be. The lice were no longer impossible, insurmountable adversaries. Still, it didn't feel triumphant like I'd always assumed it would. It felt temporary, like a trick. Any second the scratching was going to start again, I was sure. I kept trying to pull imaginary nits from my hair, itching at phantom lice.

I wasn't just worried about myself, though. I had a child now. As soon as they were born I decided I didn't want their childhood to involve endless scratching. I didn't want their childhood to involve *any* scratching. They were going to be lice-free forever. I would succeed where my parents failed.

My kid is twelve now. Though they've caught head lice at least four times during their young, everybody-throw-your-coats-into-a-pile stage, no social worker has ever come knocking. Perhaps our skin isn't dark enough for that sort of check-in.

Naturally, every time my kid has had lice, I've caught them, too. That Ouija board was full of shit.

34 GRAMS PER DOSE

The cookies don't taste how I remember them. They're Chips Ahoy! They're triple chocolate. 170 calories per 34 grams. It usually takes at least 102 grams for me to feel like I've reached what I should probably call "proper dosage," considering how and why I consume them. I've already swallowed 510 calories by the time I realize these cookies aren't the medicine I'd hoped they'd be.

For years I've believed food would make me happy. I believed it when my mother let me take a few sloppy bites of a secret Buster Bar from Dairy Queen. I believed it when I worked at a gas station convenience store, relying on chips and chocolate to fuel my eight-hour shifts. I believe it even now that my clothes from one year ago have started constricting me, leaving pink, tender welts across my stomach, my back. I'll probably believe it again as soon as the thought of these six unfulfilling cookies slides from my short-term memory.

I am twenty-five and walking down Bloor Street West, past expensive boutiques and luxury-brand storefronts I never expect to enter. Here, broken glass and cigarette butts burned down to the filter don't line the streets. There are no boarded-up windows or doors fitted with burglar bars as there are in the neighborhoods I come from. Everything here is slick lines and polished marble. Nothing conflicts with the fantasy.

Except me.

I turn to my close friend who is walking with me, telling me about a wedding she's just attended. She hovers over details of the catering, describing dishes that sound foreign to me. I shrug, say I've never tried them but if she says they're good, I trust her.

"You've never had foie gras?" she asks in disbelief.

"No. I grew up poor."

"So did I."

She has told me about her childhood poverty before. She has a very specific memory of her family combing the beach for beer bottles to take back to the liquor store so they'd have money for food. But to look at her now you'd never guess. Her skin is flawless and pale as a Southern belle's. Her hair is perfect. I've never noticed so much as a split end. It's always brushed to brilliance, or tied back simply and elegantly, or sometimes woven around her head in an intricate up-do. Her clothes are perfect. They're never stained, never torn, never hemmed sloppily. If she's wearing something that looks like silk, don't bother asking. It's definitely real silk. Her vocabulary, her manner of speaking, her delivery of smart jokes as coolly and effortlessly as a '40s femme fatale, all of it sounds and looks like money.

And then there's her extensive knowledge of culinary delicacies like foie gras. Times like this I remember poverty was an unsavoury pit stop in her life, not the final destination.

For the most part I don't feel ashamed of my poor upbringing. Of course, it's easier to detach that shame now that I'm safely outside of it. What do I have to be ashamed of now? I have running water and the ability to buy fast food whenever I want.

But when she asks me if I've ever had foie gras, her voice first so incredulous, then so dismissive, that small ember of shame that has been quietly smouldering all these years catches flame once more. I become intensely aware of my clothes, which I can only afford to buy second-hand, and which fit strangely, the way designers seem to think all plus-sized clothing should. I become aware of my shoes, which are dirty and torn. I become aware of my hair, a mass of frizzy, unruly chaos I've inherited from my mother. I, who survived on peanut butter and food-bank cereal during my formative years, who never had the good sense to develop a more expensive palate once I left home, have no business in this neighbourhood, casually perusing the windows of Dolce & Gabbana and Louis Vuitton. *Foie gras* is more than just two French words I can barely pronounce, more than just a meal certain people sometimes enjoy. It is a test that separates the high from the low, the rich from the poor, the worldly from the ignorant. The white from everyone else.

Foie gras is a test, and I have failed. Again.

When I lived on the Six Nations rez as a teen, food options were limited. There was a Zehrs grocery store in Caledonia, about seventeen kilometres away in one direction, and a few grocery stores in Brantford, about twenty kilometres away in the other. On the rez itself, we had a couple of restaurants.

140

My favourites were Village Pizza, which is basically a culinary landmark on Six Nations, and Village Café, which still serves up the best breakfast around.

But you can't subsist solely on delivery pizza and restaurant breakfast. Or at least, you shouldn't. That left gas station convenience stores to fill the culinary gap. Like any convenience store, they carried everyday staples like milk, eggs and bread, but other than that their aisles were filled with junk food and canned goods. If you were lucky, one of the gas stations might have some bananas or apples for sale, but most didn't, and nearly everything was priced higher than what you'd find at a grocery store in the city. So not only was it harder to eat healthy on the rez; it also cost more to eat unhealthy.

Our family's diet consisted mainly of low-grade ground beef and cheap pasta. Spaghetti and meatballs, Hamburger Helper, hamburgers, goulash — which, along with stuffed cabbage, was the only reminder we had of my mother's Hungarian heritage. We'd often have pancakes for supper, or, if Mom either wasn't feeling up to cooking or was in the hospital, bowls of corn flakes from the food bank, piled so high with sugar that by the time we reached the bottom of

141

the bowl the milk and sugar had formed a thick slurry.

My siblings and I self-medicated with sugar and junk food the way some self-medicate with alcohol and drugs. We might not have been able to help our mother deal with her bipolar disorder; we might not have been able to help our father shoulder the financial burden of caring for five children; we might not have had running water or a house that we'd be comfortable bringing friends to, but we did have sugar, the one luxury we could afford to indulge, the only path to normal that we could see open, inviting us in. Other kids — richer kids, off-rez kids, happy kids — had Snickers bars and Doritos and Oreos, and so, sometimes, did we.

America's food industry is highly unethical, even cruel.

This is the main takeaway of Robert Kenner's 2008 documentary *Food, Inc.* A segment titled "The Dollar Menu" profiles the Gonzalez family from California. They're hardworking, with both parents putting in long hours at unforgiving jobs to support their two children. Neither parent has enough time to really cook. The segment opens with Mr. Gonzalez ordering food for dinner from Burger King. He buys five Rodeo Cheeseburgers, two chicken sandwiches, two small Sprites and one large Dr Pepper.

The total for all that food, with tax, is $11.48, or a meagre $2.87 per person. As Mr. Gonzalez passes everything out and the family starts to eat, Mrs. Gonzalez's voice narrates: "We didn't even think about healthy eating because we used to think everything was healthy. Now that I know that the food is really unhealthy for us, I feel guilty giving it to my kids."

The movie cuts to the Gonzalez family grocery shopping. The younger daughter wants a pear. They're on sale for 99 cents per pound.

"First check to see how many are there for a pound," her mother says before walking off to join her husband.

The older sister grabs one and puts it on the scale. Her face is impassive, the way your face gets when you're used to poverty's heartbreak. The way it gets when you spend your life watching, helpless, as your parents struggle against an unrelenting tide, knowing the day will come when you must navigate that stormy sea yourself.

"Not worth it, honey," she says to her younger sister. "You can only get, like, two

143

or three."

She places a hand on the back of her sister's head and leads her away. The little girl may not understand now, but one day she'll learn, the way all poor kids must. Poor people can't afford good health. Poor people can't even afford five-cent plastic bags. My family certainly couldn't. Dad always sent us searching for empty cardboard boxes we could use instead. We'd scour the shelves for any box we could empty quickly. We'd dig through bins full of cardboard that management kept at the front of the cheapest grocery stores, knowing families like ours wouldn't waste money on plastic bags. We couldn't even if we wanted to. Every nickel counts when you're poor.

When I was a kid I thought grocery shopping was exciting. There were so many colourful boxes calling out to me, so many empty calories jockeying for their chance to be ground between my increasingly porous, cavity-riddled teeth. By the time I was eight I knew better than to ask my parents to buy me anything, but my little brother Jon was only four, so he still had hope. He would grab the brightest box with the most sugar inside, sheepishly show it to our mother, then when she shook her head and told him to put it back, say, "That's okay. Maybe next time," not daring, even at four years old, to let his disappointment weigh on her. Somehow, he'd already learned what poverty meant, how it shaped your needs, your desires, your expectations. All before he'd entered kindergarten.

The reason junk food is so much cheaper than nutritious food is the U.S. government. This is not a conspiracy theory; it's a fact. The U.S. government subsidizes what are called "cash crops": wheat, corn and soybeans. They push farmers to overproduce these crops, which farmers then sell at a deep discount to companies that turn them into high-fructose corn syrup, hydrolyzed soy protein, refined carbohydrates — all the primary ingredients in food poor families rely upon, both in Canada and in the U.S.

Since empty calories are both cheap and widely available, it should be no surprise that the biggest indicator of obesity is a person's income level. And since so many Western countries are built on white supremacy, it should also come as no surprise that the biggest indicator of poverty is race. In Canada, a staggering one in five racialized families live in poverty, as opposed to one in twenty white families. Among Americans, white people have the lowest poverty rates in the country at 9 percent. American Indian/Alaska Native people have the highest rates of poverty at 24 percent, followed closely by Black people at 22 percent and Latinx people at 19 percent. Asian people, Native Hawaiians and Pacific Islanders, who were all lumped together in this survey, experience an 11 percent poverty rate. This means many poor, racialized families are put in the position where they have no choice *but* to rely on cheap, unhealthy food and, as a result, support the same companies that have converted their poverty into corporate profit in the first place.

By encouraging farmers to overproduce cash crops, the U.S. government has ultimately helped corporations create a food economy where poor, racialized communities depend upon unhealthy food to survive. And because poor diet has been linked to health problems such as type 2 diabetes, heart problems, cancer and stroke, this would also mean that the U.S. government has been essentially paying for poor, racialized people to become sick through its crop subsidy program. In some ways this is to be expected. Capitalism always prioritizes profit over people. But it raises the question: if these crop subsidies disproportionately affected white people's health and well-being the way they disproportionately impact racialized people's health and well-being, would they still be in place?

Perhaps. Perhaps not.

In her essay "Decolonizing Empathy: Why Our Pain Will Never Be Enough to Disarm White Supremacy," Sherronda J. Brown describes a 2014 nursing book that was recalled for its descriptions of how racialized people — including "Arabs/Muslims," "Asians," "Blacks," "Jews," "Hispanics" and "Native Americans" — supposedly responded to pain. According to this book, as a Native American I can endure a very high level of pain before requesting pain meds. My husband, who has seen me pop Tylenol at even the slightest sign of a headache, would be very surprised to hear this.

The glaring omission from this list is the white race. One can assume why. For white people, other white people are considered "normal," and therefore unremarkable, meaning their pain is also "normal" and therefore unremarkable. This is how you can tell white supremacy is functioning the way it's supposed to: because white people are the standard by which all others are measured. If white people are the ones who are "normal," that means racialized people are by default "abnormal." Further, Brown argues that if white people believe Black, Indigenous and people of colour "don't feel pain in the same way that they do," then white people also "don't see us as being human in the same way that they are."

This bias is very convenient for countries like Canada and the U.S., which still have mostly white populations. If racialized people aren't considered human, it's okay for them to have unhealthy bodies. It's okay if they have unhealthy minds. It's okay if the state submits them to violence and trauma again and again and again, withholding justice and relief. All the pain white governments have historically caused racialized people can be justified; all the pain they're causing racialized people today can be justified; all the pain they will ever cause racialized people can forever be justified. After all, racialized people can't really feel pain the same way white folks can anyway.

Though American health studies have often neglected to obtain statistical facts on Indigenous people, the Canadian government has not. In fact, they've gathered information specifically about Indigenous peoples and health. In 1973, the Department of National Health and Welfare released *Nutrition Canada,* which was the result of nearly ten years of surveys on the food and nutrition of Canadians. As Krista Walters points out in her paper, " 'A National Priority': Nutrition Canada's *Survey* and the Disciplining of Aboriginal Bodies, 1964–1975," the nutrition analysts in this survey decided to group both white settlers and immigrants into a giant group they called the "national population." Two additional groups were counted, but excluded from this category: "Indians" and "Eskimos."

"The construction of these groupings underscores the special otherness of Aboriginal bodies," Walters writes, "and the form of data collection and conclusions drawn well illustrate that this government funded project aimed not simply to raise the standard of health in Canada but was part of the state's ongoing agenda to assimilate Aboriginal peoples."

How is gathering information specifically about Aboriginal peoples' health related to assimilation? It seems like a harmless enough venture, perhaps even beneficial considering how often statistics on Indigenous populations are conveniently ignored. However, as Walters points out, the study doesn't distinguish any other cultural,

149

religious, class or ethnic groups. Everyone other than "Indians" and "Eskimos" is lumped together as "non-descript Canadian citizenry, distinguished in the published reports only by region, age, and gender."

If the government wanted stats on Indigenous peoples' health so they could measure the effects of colonialism, intending to develop methods to counter and correct those effects, the decision to segregate Indigenous peoples from the "national population" would be completely justified. But the survey itself did not consider the effects reserves, the Indian Act, and residential schools have had on traditional diets and food knowledge. Nor did it consider the limited access to fresh food on reserves, or the higher costs of food on reserves compared with in urban centres.

Instead, accessible Indigenous foods like wild game, tubers, berries, wild rice and fish were considered "country food" and treated as "limited and supplementary." Certain methods of preparing food were called "primitive," a word that has been very effectively used throughout history to delegitimize Indigenous peoples' knowledge and culture. Essentially, Walters writes, if any person practised food preparation or relied on nutrition that deviated from the norms of settler Canadians, they were "patholo-gized as practising poor nutrition."

We must consider this in context. By the 1960s, people within the Canadian government were well aware of their policies of starvation used to clear the plains. They were aware of the way residential schools starved and malnourished Indigenous children in their care. They were aware of policies they had written and enforced that prohibited Indigenous people from participating in traditional hunting and fishing on their own territory. They also knew that they had forced many Indigenous communities to relocate to completely different lands, making it sometimes impossible to rely on food sources that may have been abundant before, but were scarce in their new homes.

These are only a handful of government policies that have targeted Indigenous bodies, all of which have had devastating effects on our health. By ignoring these policies but emphasizing their effects, the Canadian government's survey makes Indigenous people seem inherently unhealthy. And if we as Indigenous people are inherently unhealthy, well then, we're going to need Canada's help to become healthy again, aren't we? We might have to come live in cities, where there's more access to fresh fruits and vegetables. We might have to give up our lands and treaty rights. We might have to watch as inherently healthy Canadians move onto our homelands and build houses and grocery stores and set up farmers' markets and community gardens. We might have to pretend the very colonialism that has cursed us will suddenly, inexplicably, save us.

It's all in our best interest, really.

Whenever I looked at the food pyramid in school I was both confused and amazed. How could anyone eat three to five servings of vegetables in a day? Each member of my family only ever had one heaping spoonful of canned vegetables per day. Soft and salty string beans or mushy boiled carrots or peas like deflating balloons.

There's a certain shame in learning about the food pyramid when you're poor. Just like Canada's nutrition survey in the 1960s, teachers who preach the gospel of the food pyramid assume that if you're eating unhealthily, you have a choice. That if you're eating unhealthily, it's entirely your fault. I felt this shame acutely when I was in high school. We had to track our food for a few days in health class to measure our diet against what we were supposed to be eating according to the food pyramid. My diet, like the diets of so many poor and racialized families, consisted mostly of carbs, dairy and fat. There was very little protein, fibre, fruits or vegetables. As I filled out the worksheets, I knew that I was failing, that my family was failing. I lied to make myself seem healthier, adding tallies of fresh fruit and protein where really there was none. None of the worksheets mentioned that healthy food was more expensive, or that food banks mostly relied on giving out non-perishables to families like mine, families that visited at least one food bank every month, our hands outstretched, hoping for boxes of cereal and day-old doughnuts. In the photocopied utopia of these worksheets, there was no poverty. There were only these facts:

Fats, Oils and Sweets: use sparingly
Milk, Yogurt and Cheese: 2–3 servings
Meat, Poultry, Fish, Dry Beans, Eggs and
Nuts: 2–3 servings
Vegetables: 3–5 servings
Fruits: 2–4 servings
Bread, Cereal, Rice and Pasta: 6–11 serv-
ings

I'd stare at the list and try to imagine what

it would be like to be that well fed. For the first year and a half of high school I didn't eat anything for lunch. My dad had inquired about enrolling me in a government-subsidized lunch program, which I'd relied on for hot lunches when we lived in the States. They didn't have anything like that in Canada, though. My dad never told me this with words. I only figured it out when I saw him focus on my younger brothers, whom he now had to pack lunches for every day — something he'd never had to do, or budget for, before. He knew the teachers' attention would be on my brothers' lunch-boxes, not mine; that if they weren't prop-erly filled, social services could bang down our door and take my brothers away. I knew this was my father's biggest fear: his children disappearing into the foster care system. I could see it in his eyes when he ran to the convenience store first thing in the morning to buy peanut butter for their lunches, or, when he realized peanut butter was no longer allowed in schools, small microwav-able cans of ravioli.

I was thirteen, though. Practically an adult. I had to fend for myself. A few times a week my friend Amber took pity on me and would buy me some twelve-cent donut holes to hold me over, or a thirty-five-cent pizza bun from the grocery store across the street. My real daily food pyramid — the one I would have filled out if I hadn't been too ashamed — remained mostly empty and always unhealthy. No one seemed to notice or care. It was probably safer that way, considering what happened to the poor Native kids who *were* noticed. After all, according to teachers and social workers, journalists and politicians, neighbours and total strangers, the parents who could check off the proper boxes on the food pyramid were the only ones who really deserved children anyway.

The first time I went to my future husband Mike's house, in eleventh grade, I took one look at their stocked cupboards, the fruits on their kitchen table, their two full freezers, and I thought he and his single mother were rich. Patty was on disability due to her epilepsy and worked part-time caring for disabled children. The government deducted her income from her monthly disability cheque, so it didn't help all that much. In other words, Patty was definitely not rich. She was just smart enough to stock up on food when it was on sale.

Patty had picked up this stockpiling technique from her mother, Betty. Betty often went hungry as a child because her parents thought the men in the family needed food more than she did. They lived on a farm, and though her brothers were supposed to be doing chores and manual labour, proving their masculine worth, Betty was often the one left doing everything, her stomach concave, empty.

When I found out about this, I couldn't help but think of my family. While I know my parents' focus on my brothers' lunches wasn't a deliberate attempt to starve me, I also know that both Betty's parents and my own had a choice to make, and we were the ones who lost. How many families must make that choice? How many children must lose?

Sometimes I wonder whether Betty binged on food once she started making her own money, the way I did once I had a job. Whether she, too, tried to fill her stomach to bursting to make up for all the times it wasn't full in her youth.

Maybe it was just me.

It is only recently that Canada's treatment of Indigenous peoples has been referred to as genocide, and even then, it's usually been "cultural genocide," as if that somehow softens its edges and makes it more permissible. More Canadian. I suppose, though, when one considers America's 2009 "Apology to Native Peoples of the United States," which was quietly passed through Congress attached to a 67-page military spending bill, and boiled down systematic, intentional genocide of Indigenous men, women and children to the much more tepidly described "violence, maltreatment and neglect," or even worse, mere "conflict," genocide is not really the sort of thing any country is eager to admit to.

Brent Bezo, in *The Impact of Intergenerational Transmission of Trauma from the Holodomor Genocide of 1932–1933 in Ukraine,* describes how the Holodomor, a forced starvation that killed millions of Ukrainians, undermined its victims' lives:

[Holodomor survivors] reported that the confiscation of food, personal property and homes rendered them "bare" and resulted in the complete loss of traditional means to independently support, look after, and maintain themselves and their families. This loss was reported as a "destruction" of independent self-sufficiency that was a "deliberate act to break the will of the Ukrainian people" and "to show people" "that they would not become independent Ukrainian people."

When I first read that my breath caught in my throat. Never before had I seen a non-Indigenous person so succinctly sum up the way that my people's experience of genocide worked. First, remove the means for the people to independently look after and support themselves and their community. Next, force them to become dependent upon the very state that wants to destroy them. Withhold basic necessities. Wait.

This is the exact tactic Canada and the U.S. have used on Indigenous peoples for hundreds of years. So many of our nations have been forcefully displaced, so many of our children stolen from our arms and placed in residential schools or, more recently, in the arms of overworked social workers and violent foster parents, as if white abuse could ever be better than Indigenous love. These policies are not about what's best for Indigenous peoples, despite repeated claims of faux concern from government officials. These policies are about what's best for Canada and the U.S. They are the reason Indigenous peoples have control over only 0.02 percent of our original lands in Canada, and 2 percent of our original lands in the U.S. — a meagre amount that is still, according to some, too much. Colonial success has always depended upon Indigenous destruction.

Just as genocide tends to use the same tactics from country to country to carry out its horrors, genocide also tends to produce similar effects in the lives of survivors. In Bezo's study, he discusses the discrepancies between what could be called Ukraine's successes and what could be called its failures, years after the Holodomor. For instance, Ukraine is one of Europe's fastest-growing economies and is ranked fourth in the world for its adult literacy rate. Yet, out of forty-one countries, Ukraine has the highest percentage of eleven-, thirteen- and fifteen-year-olds who drink alcohol at least once a week. It has the second-highest number of eleven-year-olds who get drunk at least once a week, and the most eleven-year-olds who smoke at least once a week. It holds the unfortunate title of lowest life expectancy in Europe.

How can a country be doing so well economically and educationally and still be suffering so acutely? Something as traumatic as genocide doesn't have a definitive ending point. Its horrors live on in the memories of those who survive, playing over and over with no reprieve. What are you supposed to do once you know the depths of human suffering? Once you've experienced the limits of human depravity and indifference? Once you've witnessed how easy it was for people, neighbours even, to see you and your family as less than human, to treat you as less than human, or to look the other way and let it happen? How do you take that knowledge and try to continue on the same way you did before? Everything has a different taste, a different tone. No amount of economic or educational success can change that.

And yet some seem to think it can. In both Canada and the U.S., Indigenous people exhibit many of the same behaviours as post-Holodomor Ukrainians, a fact Bezo acknowledges in his study. We have statistically higher levels of heavy drinking than non-Indigenous Canadians. Those of us who live in America and drink are substantially more likely to be problem or excessive drinkers. We have a five- to ten-year lower life expectancy, depending on gender in Canada. Our men in America have the lowest life expectancy of all men, and our women have a death rate that has gone up 20 percent in 15 years. During this same period, the overall death rate in America has decreased by 17 percent. Even worse, while the infant mortality rate in America has gone down overall, the death rate for Native babies in America has increased by an outrageous 44 percent from 1999-2009. Our rates of daily smoking are almost double that of non-Indigenous Canadians. In the U.S. we have the highest rate of smoking, over all other races and ethnic groups. The only thing Indigenous people in North America and Ukrainians have in common — the only thing that could account for these eerily similar stats — are our respective experiences of genocide.

I've read so many angry comments degrading Indigenous people because we haven't been as economically and educationally successful as those who haven't experienced genocide. Or because, according to these people, Jewish Holocaust survivors have overcome their genocide better than we have, so we must be inherently deficient. I've heard people say Indigenous people need to "get over" our genocide, as though it's not still happening now in newer, more socially acceptable ways. Would making more money and being more literate make us more deserving of human compassion? It certainly wouldn't remove our pain; after all, Ukraine's economic and educational successes haven't made its citizens' intergenerational trauma magically disappear.

Epigenetics is the study of how a person's actions and experiences can affect their genetic makeup, causing certain genes to become either active or dormant. It's a term that was coined by scientists Lars Olov Bygren and Marcus Pembrey to describe the results they observed in four scientific studies they conducted, both separately and together, which could not otherwise be explained by modern genetics. Two of the studies were of Överkalix, a secluded Swedish community whose seasons of feast or famine were based almost entirely on the success of their barley and rye harvests. Bygren and Pembrey found that the granddaughters of women who were in the womb during famine seasons, and were therefore undernourished when their eggs were forming, had a significantly increased risk of early death compared with those whose grandmothers did not experience famine in utero. This finding supported an earlier study Bygren did on Överkalix, which found grandsons of men who experienced a feast season prior to puberty — the time when their sperm were developing — and therefore overate, were also significantly more likely to die an early death due to diabetes or heart failure. The scientists found similarly puzzling results when studying the effects of smoking: the sons of 166 English men who smoked before puberty were consistently fatter than the sons of men who either hadn't smoked at all or had started smoking after puberty.

There was no scientific reason this should be the case — no DNA sequences had changed — yet it clearly was. The evidence was all there, suggesting that not only a person's environment but also their individual decisions could alter the expression of their genes and thus influence the lives of their descendants.

Haudenosaunee have always believed in the principle of the seven generations. When you make a decision, you must consciously think about what effects that decision could have on your descendants seven generations in the future. This world does not belong to you; you are merely borrowing it from the coming faces. Epigenetics seems to replicate that philosophy on the genetic level. Your decisions and traumas are never solely yours alone, or even yours and your children's. Your decisions and traumas mark every subsequent generation after you, creating ripples in the future that can't always be anticipated and can never be controlled.

What does this mean for those who experienced starvation, malnutrition and other forms of trauma in residential schools?

What does this mean for their children, grandchildren, great-grandchildren? Historian of food, health and colonialism Ian Mosby and assistant professor of anthropology at the University of Toronto Tracey Galloway have looked at some of these ramifications in their article " 'Hunger Was Never Absent': How Residential School Diets Shaped Current Patterns of Diabetes among Indigenous Peoples in Canada." The quote in the title comes from residential school survivor Russell Moses, who used it to describe his years in Brantford, Ontario's Mohawk Institute. One can see why he said this — and also why survivors referred to the school as "the Mush Hole" — when looking at its menu on any given day:

Breakfast consisted of "two slices of bread with either jam or honey as the dressing, oatmeal with worms or corn meal porridge, which was minimal in quantity and appalling in quality." For lunch, it was "water as the beverage . . . one and a half slices of *dry* bread, and the main course consisted of a 'rotten soup' . . . (i.e., scraps of beef, vegetables, some in a state of decay)." For supper, "students were given two slices of bread and jam, fried potatoes, *no meat* [and] a bun baked by the girls." Moses even recalled hungry children "eating from the swill barrel, picking out soggy bits of food that was intended for the pigs."

Moses's experience was hardly the exception. As Mosby and Galloway note, hunger was so prevalent inside residential schools that, between 1948 and 1952, more than a thousand malnourished students from six residential schools were used as subjects for nutrition experiments. Instead of being helped, these children were treated as perfect specimens for scientific inquiry. Their pain was measured and mapped, theorized about and eventually immortalized in cold, clinical reports.

I wonder what these scientists told themselves when they conducted their experiments, how they rationalized their complicity. Whether they thought about these children while eating their breakfast in the morning, or breaking from work for lunch. Whether they considered themselves lucky to find so many starving Indigenous children to experiment on. Whether they were, in some ways, thankful Canada both mandated and drastically underfunded residential schools, because it made finding malnourished test subjects that much easier. Or whether they ignored these types of thoughts altogether, because coming face to face with what they meant would shatter everything they believed about their country, about themselves.

The physiological effects of starving follow a person for the rest of their life. Mosby and Galloway cite studies that show that childhood hunger often causes stunted height, which in turn can cause an increased tendency towards obesity as well as higher rates of developing type 2 diabetes. Metabolic changes occur, as well, which means that even when a child is no longer starving, hunger has essentially trained the body to continue to accumulate more fat regardless. Given these sorts of impacts on residential school survivors, combined with what we are learning about the ways epigenetics passes these experiences on, how can we possibly expect survivors' descendants to be much better off? To "get over" a genocide that has marked their very genes, and their children's genes, and *their* children's genes?

My paternal grandmother, Melita Elliott, did not attend the Mush Hole. A well-off

Mohawk family from my community sent their kids to get educated in the United States, then, when they came back to Six Nations, they opened schools themselves, offering an alternative to the residential school. That's where my grandmother went — to a numbered school. She was the only child in her family who went. Her siblings weren't so lucky.

I know very little about my paternal grandfather, Arthur Elliott. But I know there are Elliotts who did attend the Mush Hole. I saw their names on a graduation list during a tour. I felt like I was going to vomit.

My father, thankfully, did not attend the Mush Hole. His mother moved their entire family to Buffalo, New York, to make sure he and his siblings would be safe. I can't imagine the fear or resolve it would take to make such a decision, if one can call it a decision. My grandmother could either become a refugee on her own people's lands or watch the Mush Hole swallow her children one by one.

Mosby and Galloway write, "We can now be fairly certain that the elevated risk of obesity, early-onset insulin resistance and diabetes observed among Indigenous peoples in Canada arises, in part at least, from the prolonged malnutrition experienced by many residential school survivors." My father has diabetes. One of his sisters and one of his brothers have diabetes. Their mother had diabetes. I haven't developed diabetes yet, but I often feel it's only a matter of time before my insulin levels drop and my diagnosis comes in. It's my genetic inheritance.

My kid's, too.

The ways Indigenous peoples deal with our trauma, whether with alcohol or violence or Chips Ahoy! cookies, get pathologized under colonialism. Instead of looking at the horrors Canada has inflicted upon us and linking them to our current health issues, Canada has chosen to blame our biology, as though those very genes they're blaming weren't marked by genocide, too. This is how a once thriving, healthy population comes to be "inherently unhealthy." It wasn't the genocide that centuries of Canadian officials enacted upon us that was the problem; it was how we reacted to that genocide. It was our fault, our bodies' faults.

Abusers rarely take responsibility for themselves. They prefer to blame their victims for their actions.

The first time I made Hamburger Helper it

was because my mother was in the hospital. She usually cooked every day, but she was either too depressed or too manic for Dad to tolerate anymore, so he had her committed. He was selling satellite dish subscriptions door to door at the time. He came home tired, too tired to worry about cooking. I was eleven or twelve. Old enough to figure it out.

No one had taught me to cook, so all I had were the instructions on the box. I had no idea I was supposed to thaw the ground beef, so I plopped the frozen chunk in the frying pan and turned on the stove. As soon as the bottom was done I flipped it over, patiently scraped the cooked portion away with a wooden spoon, waited for the bottom to cook again, then repeated the process until everything was brown and broken apart. It took almost a half-hour.

I added the water, the noodles, the flavoured powder, hoping that dinner would taste like Mom had made it. She was often an inattentive cook, either serving crunchy, uncooked noodles or noodles boiled to mush, so the bar wasn't exactly high. But Mom's love and attention were what my siblings and I hungered for most, anyway, and that was never something I could recreate for them in her absence, no matter how hard I tried.

In *My Conversations with Canadians,* Stō:lo writer and Indigenous literary icon Lee Maracle shares a reaction she had to an Indigenous dance performance called *Agua/ Water.* Though in front of her eyes there was dancing, she says, "In my mind, I watched my grandmothers, my great-grandmothers, hauling McClary stoves across mountain passes, digging clams whose beds were dying, poisoned by toxic waste that was not to be cleaned up for over a hundred years. I watched them feed children consumed with disease and I grieved as I imagined who we might have been if, when the interlopers came, we had been invited back to the table they appropriated from our Ta'ahs." When I think back to that first time I cooked for my family, I think of Maracle's words. The food that night was edible, so technically it was fine. But I wonder what the first meal I cooked would have been if poverty, violence, mental illness and trauma hadn't kept my family in a sort of permanent survival mode. Would my mother have had the time to teach me how to thaw ground beef? Would she have taught me how to make a salad, a simple task that still, for some reason, intimidates me? Would my father have known how to hunt? How to properly skin a deer and tan a hide? Would he have known better than to plant an entire field of fruits and vegetables — white corn, tomatoes, cucumbers, strawberries — on the land across the creek from our trailer, where it flooded every year without fail, destroying all but the hardiest, most stubborn plants?

Would my grandmother have taught me how to properly make frybread, told me how sticky the dough should be, how long it should be left under the yellow, bubbling oil? Would my aunts have taught me how to plant the three sisters in traditional Haudenosaunee mounds? The corn steady and strong in the middle, beans stealthily climbing its stalks, and the squash spread out around them both, protecting them from weeds and pests? Those three crops alone had enough nutritional value to sustain our people on a vegetarian diet. Would we all be lean, strong and healthy if we still lived on that today?

Maybe if circumstances were different, if history were different, if trauma hadn't tattooed itself across my genes, I would be able to move around my kitchen with ease, knowing exactly what foods I should cook for my family and exactly how to cook them. Maybe I'd know the land the way my ancestors wanted me to know it, care for it tenderly, lovingly, the way a child is supposed to care for their mother.

Maybe I wouldn't rely on sugary food to see me through my battles with anxiety and depression, forever chasing the temporary bliss of that first sweet bite.

My mother loved Smartfood white cheddar popcorn with the same dangerous ferocity she loved my father. Any time she had an extra couple bucks, she'd pick up a big bag, which she ate fast and furious. Once she swallowed a handful of kernels so quickly she started choking, and rather than stop eating so she could get her throat clear she threw another handful of popcorn in her mouth.

"What are you doing!" my siblings and I yelled. "Stop eating! You're choking!"

We were incredulous, not sure whether to laugh at the absurdity or cover our mouths in horror. We ended up laughing, as my family tends to do. Even my mother laughed once she'd stopped coughing. My siblings and I still bring this memory up from time to time. "What was Mom thinking?" we ask one another, delirious with laughter, our eyes leaking tears.

How do we break down this cycle of intergenerational trauma and ill health? By making enough money to afford healthy food, and by ensuring our children become wealthy enough to afford healthy food, too? By moving to well-off neighbourhoods in populated cities, where food insecurity isn't an issue? Capitalism forever positions itself as the solution to the problem of capitalism. Colonialism forever positions itself as the solution to the problem of colonialism. As though shovelling more of what we're currently choking on into our mouths would ever actually help us.

I wanted to end this essay with hope, but for a long time I wasn't sure how. My experiences with food have been dysfunctional, and though I can identify that dysfunction, I still haven't figured out how to change it. How can I offer hope for others when I can't find it for myself? When we're facing a colonial history that has altered our very DNA?

Recently I read a Facebook post from nêhiyaw writer, activist and self-described philosopher queen Erica Violet Lee, who said, "If historical trauma is strong enough to alter our DNA and remain in our bones for generations, then there is no question in my mind that the love of our ancestors is in our DNA and our bones as well. The memory of that love is strong enough that it still exists in us, and in the plants that we have always cared for."

Food that carries the love of our ancestors *can* be medicine — a medicine that offers something much stronger than whatever temporary feelings of control or relief I've experienced bingeing on triple-chocolate cookies. Corn, beans and squash were once all my people really needed. They were so essential to our everyday lives that we referred to them as our sisters. We would preserve each plant's seeds and pass them on to our children, knowing that with this gift, they would be able to provide the same nutritious food for their families that we provided for them. This was an act of absolute, undiminished intergenerational love. And if intergenerational trauma can alter DNA, why can't intergenerational love?

174

BOUNDARIES LIKE BRUISES

Our love was a process of unlearning the bad love we'd been given. I know that now. I feel it when I wipe tears from your cheek, when you hold me close and stroke my back until the sobbing spasms stop. I feel it when we stare one another's traumas down, refuse to tremble, refuse to break.

We both came from poor families, lugging legacies we never deserved. I remember the first and last time I kicked you out of anger. We were walking through the Price Chopper parking lot beside our high school. I did it in front of my sister and your best friend. You tripped me playfully. I stumbled, but didn't fall, and even as my foot connected with your shin, I thought we would somehow end up laughing. Men getting hurt was funny. Men getting hurt was normal.

You didn't laugh. You asked what was wrong with me, and I pretended not to know. But I knew. Trauma and silence flanked me like foot soldiers, only they weren't doing my bidding; I was doing theirs.

You've never hit me, kicked me, pushed me, punched me. You've barely even sworn at me. Sometimes I wonder how you conjured up your version of manhood. You had no father you knew, no grandfathers. You had professional wrestling during its most misogynistic era and a couple Blink-182 albums. Neither were particularly revolutionary when it came to their depictions of masculinity.

That's not to say we've fully shrugged off the roles we've been assigned. You are a man; I am a woman. You are a settler; I'm Onkwehon:we. These differences are stakes in our ground, mapping boundaries that feel like bruises. Any time we push against them it hurts, but we both know we must be more than historical vessels, holding pain; more than performers reenacting ancient scripts. Despite our best efforts, different shades of abuse will still colour our interactions — sometimes soft and diluted like watercolours, sometimes harsh and angry like charcoal. Cycles are hard to break.

My parents never broke theirs; after twenty years, the cycle broke them. Moving to the Six Nations reserve did it. Suddenly, my white mother became the minority. For the first time she felt her whiteness — no longer a shield but a siren, screaming inherited histories she'd either never been taught or been forced to forget. Any time my father tried to connect with his Haudenosaunee culture she felt it: her whiteness blinding and bright, as if a spotlight were shone on her.

She wasn't racist. She couldn't be. She had a Native husband, Native children. She lived on a reserve. And yet her white fragility and Catholic colonialism were racist. She wasn't happy when my father finally felt pride in his brown skin. She felt wounded, excluded. She accused him of being racist against whites. She accused him of committing a mortal sin: turning his back on the Catholic Church he'd only joined to appease her.

I learned three things watching my mother:

1. No one can fuck their way to tolerance.
2. No one can marry into tolerance.
3. No one can carry for nine months and give birth to tolerance.

I've learned more watching you. You don't

flinch when I say the word "white." You don't feel attacked when I discuss colonialism. You encourage me to spend time with my family and community, to learn my language, to stand up for my people, to stand up for our land. You encourage our child to do the same. You see me as a Haudenosaunee woman, love me as a Haudenosaunee woman, and don't feel threatened by what that means.

I remember when my father first taught me about the Two Row Wampum. It was originally a treaty between the Haudenosaunee and the Dutch, but it was accepted by the Crown, and therefore by Canada. They've never been able to uphold it.

It's a belt of white wampum beads, representing the river of life. There are two rows of purple wampum that travel through the centre. One row represents the ship the settlers are steering; the other represents the canoe the Haudenosaunee are steering. Each vessel holds those peoples' culture, language, history and values. The boat and canoe go down the river of life together — parallel but never touching, never crossing into the other's path, never attempting to steer the other's vessel or interfere with the other's responsibilities. Neither vessel is better than the other. Neither group can make decisions for the other. It is a treaty based on peace and friendship, anchored in a deep respect for each culture's distinct differences.

Because of you, I understand how the Two Row Wampum can be more than just a treaty between two nations of people; it can be a lived treaty between two individuals, between us: a Haudenosaunee woman and a settler man. These boundaries don't have to be bruises. They can be our strength.

We untangle the threads of history and treat the wounds we find underneath. We listen to one another, support one another, resist our impulses to rewrite one another, to steer one another. We try to understand our distinct physical, emotional, spiritual and mental needs and meet them as best we can.

Antiracism is a process. Decolonial love is a process. Our love is a process. I never want it to end.

ON FORBIDDEN ROOMS AND INTENTIONAL FORGETTING

Once upon a time there was a man named Bluebeard, a man so wealthy he was able to buy a string of young wives. None of the relationships worked out. Still, Bluebeard was persistent. His latest acquisition was a girl who did not want to marry him but who was dragged down the aisle nonetheless.

Shortly after their marriage, Bluebeard announced to his wife that he had to leave on urgent business. He told her to enjoy her time without him, then handed over a ring of keys. She could use any of the keys, he said — all except one: a small, rusted key to a closet on the first floor. He led her to the door, then warned her: "Never open this door or you shall suffer my wrath."

Though she initially tried to resist, the young wife was so overcome with curiosity that she had to open the forbidden door. Inside were the dead, mutilated bodies of all his former wives. As soon as Bluebeard came back he knew she'd opened the door.

"You must now face my wrath," he told her, "and join my other wives." Naturally, before he could kill his wife, her strapping brothers arrived out of nowhere and killed Bluebeard. His young wife inherited his fortune. Apparently she lived happily ever after — whatever that means.

I've always been confused by the moral of this French folktale. Charles Perrault, who wrote the most famous iteration of the Bluebeard story, suggests the following interpretation: "Curiosity, in spite of its appeal, often leads to deep regret. To the displeasure of many a maiden, its enjoyment is short lived. Once satisfied, it ceases to exist, and always costs dearly." According to Perrault, it seems we're supposed to shame Bluebeard's wife for her curiosity. The problem with that, of course, is Bluebeard was a serial killer. Behind that forbidden door were dead women. If she hadn't used that key, are we supposed to believe that Bluebeard would have treated her well and grown old with her? That he would have stopped killing altogether? Somehow I doubt that.

Perrault's failure to mention the sins of Bluebeard is suspicious, to say the least. Why doesn't his moral caution against doing terrible things that become terrible

181

secrets? Against not only murdering your wives but foolishly hoping their bodies would be safe in your first-floor closet forever? If the roles of Bluebeard and his wife were swapped, I have a feeling this would be the case. Bluebeard wouldn't be shamed for being curious. He would be lifted up as a hero: the man who bravely opened the door his wife demanded stay shut, finally revealing her as the murderous, manipulative witch she always was.

The real moral of this story, the one Perrault is too cowardly to admit, is that secrets are allowed to be kept only if they are a man's secrets. The woman who threatens to reveal those secrets will live a life of deep regret. Any enjoyment she may experience will be short lived and cost her dearly.

When I was sexually assaulted I didn't tell anyone. I didn't even let myself think the words "sexual assault." My bodily reactions — constant stress, crying, disordered eating and sleeping, vomiting, wanting to drink during the day and avoid all sexual contact — were screaming to me that something was very wrong, but I wilfully ignored the signs, reminding myself that I was an outspoken feminist who knew all about consent. I wasn't the type of woman who got raped.

Meanwhile, the man who sexually assaulted me was sending me threats. He warned me not to tell anyone what happened. To keep his secret. I agreed. Even when I couldn't keep his secret anymore, I still kept it. I told everyone that what happened was consensual. To this day, I've only ever told three people the truth.

It didn't matter. He was furious. He retaliated by telling my best friend at the time an awful story, the details of which I still don't know. She refused to speak to me for weeks. When she finally responded to my texts it was only to tell me to stop texting my rapist. I hadn't messaged him in days, but he was still sending me regular death threats. Apparently she hadn't asked him to stop texting me.

He'd warned me. Society had warned me. I didn't listen. Now I was facing its wrath.

In the days, weeks, months and years following my sexual assault, I've gone over the details in my head many times. I've played out alternative scenarios, tortured myself with how small changes to choices I'd made could have stopped everything. My inner logic sounds eerily similar to the logic of attorneys who represent accused rapists. I've questioned what I drank that night, what I wore, what I'd said to my rapist in every interaction leading up to then, what I'd said to him in every interaction afterwards.

The only thing that has made me feel better is actively distracting myself from remembering anything at all about that night. At first I was wary of doing this. There's a very clear stigma around repression and denial. We are constantly told that we should face our traumas and work through them. This is the correct way to heal. But every time I tried to sift sense from my guilt and pain, all I found was more guilt and pain. Eventually I decided that, little by little, and as much as I was able, I wanted to forget.

I don't want this choice to be falsely characterized as denial. I'm not denying what happened to me. I couldn't. That night represented a break between who I was and who I've become. I can no more go back to my old self than cooked food can become raw again.

But I can stop the cycle of torturing myself.

Maybe.

I can try.

Apparently, intentional forgetting is a defence mechanism, which is somehow different from a conscious coping strategy. I don't know exactly what that difference is. Even Phebe Cramer's study on the difference between the two, literally titled "Coping and Defense Mechanisms: What's the Difference?", had little to offer. One set of criteria she examined that tried to differentiate between coping and defence mechanisms was considered "more a matter of emphasis than critical difference." Another, based on how both affect psychological or physical health, was "found to be without support."

The obvious differences to me are the negative and positive connotations. Calling something a "defence mechanism" implies that the person is accidentally dealing with an issue without meaning to, whereas calling something a "coping strategy" or "coping mechanism" implies the person is choosing to deal with that issue. In other words, one is passive and one is active. Passivity is usually considered a feminine trait, and therefore undesirable. Being active, on the other hand, is considered inherently masculine, and therefore aspirational. It's strange that something like intentional forgetting, which is done actively, is still considered a passive defence mechanism. Perhaps not as strange as giving different, arguably gendered terms to the same healing process, but we are living in a society that encourages companies to take two of the same razors, paint one pink and one blue, then charge more money for the pink one. This sort of thing should probably be expected.

Though intentional forgetting is seen as a bad way to heal, there is mounting evidence that it is, in fact, a better alternative to intentionally remembering. The more that we revisit events, the more entrenched they become in our memory. When those events are traumatic, such as with a sexual assault, they have negative emotions attached to them, which are nearly impossible to separate from the memories themselves. Continually revisiting these negative memories not only keeps those memories fresh; it also keeps the person remembering them from feeling good.

This is similar to the way that depression works. As Jutta Joormann, Paula T. Hertel, Faith Brozovich and Ian H. Gotlib explain in their study "Remembering the Good,

Forgetting the Bad: Intentional Forgetting of Emotional Material in Depression," depressed people have a tendency to almost continually reflect on their past. Their tendency to not only dwell on past events but conjure up negative thoughts and memories creates a cycle of negativity they cannot seem to escape:

> At the same time that depressed individuals hold positive beliefs about rumination as a coping strategy, they hold negative beliefs about the uncontrollability of rumination. Thus, depressed individuals might deliberately engage in rumination in an attempt to solve their problems but then become overwhelmed by negative thoughts about their ruminations.

They conclude that a depressed person's tendency to dwell on negative memories and thoughts instead of actively suppressing them is an unfortunate, cyclical part of depression. Further, they suggest training depressed people to intentionally forget "could prove to be an effective strategy."

Maybe trying to forget your trauma isn't as unhealthy as we thought.

Let me be clear: I'm not encouraging

survivors of sexual assault to stay silent. It's very important that survivors disclose what happened to them to people they trust, so those people can support the survivor in whatever ways they need. But the amount of detail that we go into when we decide to disclose our assault should always be up to us.

It's natural to have questions for sexual assault survivors. People may even think they're doing us a favour by persuading us to tell them everything that happened. After all, the truth supposedly sets us free. But isn't the most important truth that we were assaulted? Isn't that enough? Or must we relive our pain in agonizing detail so other people's curiosity is quenched?

I keep coming back to Bluebeard's forbidden room. I have one, too. Instead of being full of the corpses of former lovers, though, mine holds a memory of that night. It's projected on the wall in an endless loop. Every time I watch it I criticize myself mercilessly, stupidly hoping that if I watch it long enough the ending will change. Of course it never does.

I hate this room. I hate what it holds, what it makes me feel, what it makes me think. Whenever I can escape, I lock it up tight. I pass the key off to someone I trust and try to forget any of it exists.

Because I'm a woman, though, once I've handed you the key to this room, I have no control over whether you choose to open it. My secrets are never really mine.

When I was a child my mother told me about Jesus's resurrection. He told his apostles he would rise again on the third day after his death. When that third day came and he appeared to them in Galilee, Thomas didn't believe it was him. Who would believe something like that? It goes against our understanding of the world. Jesus may have been the son of God, but he was dead. He couldn't come back.

The only way Jesus could convince Thomas he was, in fact, himself was by letting him put his fingers in his open wounds. Thomas gouged the holes where nails had gone through Jesus's hands and feet, slid his own hands inside the wide gash in Jesus's side. Only when Thomas examined the evidence of his lord's pain first-hand was that pain finally made real to him. Only when Thomas felt the contours of Jesus's torture was Jesus himself made real to him. He had no problems believing once Jesus offered up his trauma as proof.

As a child, this story disturbed me. I imagined Jesus wincing with pain as Thomas examined his body, his hands emerging dripping with blackening blood. What kind of friend was he? Why did his belief hinge on such grisly proof? How did this make Jesus feel, that his best friend wouldn't believe him unless he let him violate his body?

I often wonder about this burden of proof. Is my pain valid only when someone bears witness to it? Must I be hypervigilant about my entire person, always? Make sure that my face is composed in the perfect silhouette of trauma — any hint of a smile hastily swept away — whenever I expect someone to believe me? Must I forsake all joy, all warmth, to take up my role as "perfect victim"? As if ever experiencing happiness again were somehow evidence that I never experienced agony, anguish?

Maybe this is why I've told so few people.

There is a performative nature to pain. It's never just for us; it's also for those around us. In case I happen to forget this in my own life, I have plenty of reminders. For example, the case of Amanda Knox.

Knox, a twenty-year-old American living in Perugia, Italy, returned home after spending the night with her boyfriend. She found her flatmate, Meredith Kercher, murdered and called the police. One of the lead detectives noticed that Knox was not crying hysterically, as he assumed she should be. Instead, she was kissing her boyfriend — something he reasoned that no innocent woman would ever do after her flatmate was found murdered. Her response to trauma was so far from what this detective deemed the "right" response, she became the main suspect in the murder case.

No evidence connected her to the murder. No blood, no DNA, no motive. The prosecution had to conjure up a ridiculous story that maintained that Knox somehow killed Kercher without leaving any DNA evidence, while another suspect, Rudy Guede, left DNA all over the room. It didn't matter. Knox still was convicted and imprisoned for four years before being retried and, eventually, acquitted.

If Amanda Knox had performed her trauma properly, maybe she wouldn't have been treated, tried and imprisoned as a criminal. If I'd performed my trauma properly — cried in front of family and friends, poured big glugs of vodka into my orange juice while they were watching, thrown up on their shoes instead of in the toilet of a private bathroom stall — maybe they wouldn't have been so quick to believe me when I lied and told them that I'd wanted it.

I never know when I'm allowed to feel my pain and when I must put it away for the sake of company. People may want me to cry in front of them initially, to "prove" myself, to make them feel a part of my pain, but they don't want that proof — or pain — to last forever. They don't want me to start hyperventilating while we're watching an episode of *Girls* that unexpectedly deals with rape. They certainly don't want me to ruin their outing to Banff's Cave and Basin by having a breakdown when a strange man pushes past me.

These displays are not cute. They're not "healing." They're inconvenient: intrusions of real-world ugliness that disrupt the collective illusion of perfect put-togetherness. Despite this idea that we as survivors should share, that we should remember and then move past our pain, that we should "deal" with our issues, there are very few places any of us can show our scars without being shamed. If we slip up and accidentally let our trauma overtake us in public or at the wrong moment, we are treated with shock and disdain — as though showing human emotion makes us somehow less than human.

I suppose I should stop being so surprised when we're treated as less than human. After all, the trial of Cindy Gladue's murderer was in 2015, and the levels of dehumanization the Canadian courts allowed to take place during it are enough to make a person physically ill. I would rather not go into the details of the sexual assault that led to her death, which are incredibly disturbing. Instead, I would like to emphasize that Gladue was a thirty-six-year-old Métis woman with three teenage daughters. She was struggling to overcome addiction, but she was still a person, she still experienced joy. She liked cooking shows, made legendary apple crisps, loved to draw and listen to Mötley Crüe. She sang Sarah McLachlan's "Angel" to her daughters to lull them to sleep. She was loving. She was loved.

During the trial, photos of Gladue's dead body were shown in front of her mother without warning, the disturbing image imprinted in her mind forever. Gladue's vaginal tissue, the most private part of her body, was entered into court evidence and displayed to a roomful of strangers. This was the first time human tissue had ever been accepted as evidence in a trial — an unprecedented move that was apparently required to convince an all-white jury that Gladue, an Indigenous woman who performed sex work, deserved justice when she was murdered. She still didn't get that justice. Her murderer was cleared of all charges, which meant her body was further violated after her death for no reason. Her trauma was put on display in a desperate attempt to shock jury members into feeling empathy for someone they'd been told their whole lives wasn't a real person; to remind jury members that her murderer, a white man, the type they'd been told their whole lives to make excuses and allowances for, was deserving of punishment this time instead of more excuses and allowances.

That's the unspoken truth about these pleas for our stories, and these criminal trials. They're never just a presentation of the facts. They're arguments — and one side is much easier to argue than the other. Arguing for a woman to be considered a liar in a society that has hammered in our inherent unreliability is not difficult at all. Arguing for us to be believed is much more challenging.

Similarly, arguing that a manipulative woman is making false claims of rape to get "even" with an innocent man is not hard; it's merely spitting back up the same ideas about men and women we've all been forced to swallow for centuries. But arguing that a woman deserves the right to police the boundaries of her own body — boundaries that are continually, sometimes violently broken by men who have been taught to disregard women's active, informed consent — is a task similar to Sisyphus rolling a boulder up a hill, waiting for it to roll back down and crush him. It's contrary to all that we've been taught about women and men. It questions the very legitimacy of Western misogyny, and thus, Western society.

In other words, it's blasphemy.

People are willing to believe anything that reinforces their unexamined view of the world, no matter how far it strains the laws of physics, decency and common sense. They'll believe Gladue consented to the sexual assault that ended up killing her.

They'll believe that Knox was a crime-scene mastermind able to erase only her own DNA from a murder scene. They'll believe that you, nearly blackout drunk and crawling over train tracks minutes before, were in a perfect state of mind to consent to sex, and did. And the only way to even attempt to convince them otherwise is to let them stick their fingers in your bloody wounds. Give them details you'd rather not relive. Let them see. Let them feel. Let them taste. Your comfort, consent and mental health didn't matter before. Why should they matter now? You want them to believe you, don't you? Don't you?

If we aren't required to give consent or allowed to refuse consent when it comes to recounting our own trauma, what is left for us? The men who carry out this violence against us don't have to testify in their own defence, yet we have to relive our trauma to prove our innocence. Our innocence is always what's really on trial, not these men's guilt.

I suspect men who rape don't encounter anywhere near as many questions in their daily life about what they did and why as those they raped. They don't have to watch people evaluate every last detail of their appearance, mindset, alcohol level, sexual history, actions leading up to the assault and following the assault, as they weigh whether or not to believe them. I suspect they don't have panic attacks or hyperventilate on occasions when people ask these questions. I suspect they don't even feel any guilt. After all, they were just doing what society has told them they have always had a right to do.

When I advocate for my right to forget about my sexual assault, I'm advocating for the same right my assaulter has been given. I'm advocating for people to believe me with the same blind faith people believed my assaulter. I'm advocating for the right to move on with my life, the same way my assaulter is allowed to move on with his. I'm advocating for the right to be occasionally happy, the chance to achieve my goals, to be considered more than someone's victim. Had I taken my assaulter to court, his lawyer would have made the same argument about him: that he has the right to be happy, to achieve his goals, to be considered more than someone's assaulter. That argument would more than likely get him cleared. Even though only the strongest sexual assault cases even go to trial, only 42 percent come back with a guilty verdict. Sexual assault has one of the smallest conviction rates of violent crime in Canada. The Rape, Abuse & Incest National Network (RAINN) has estimated that less than a third of rape incidents in the United States are even reported to the police. A mere 5.7 percent of rape incidents will end in arrest, with only 0.7 percent leading to felony convictions.

When you take two of the same thing and paint one pink and one blue, why does the pink one always cost more?

Here are other morals of other stories: Survivors should not have to live lives of deep regret for other people's actions.

Another person's decision to commit a crime against us should never cost us more dearly than it costs the person who committed the crime.

Our trauma is not something we should ever be expected to supply upon demand.

Healing is not the same for everyone.

My trauma is locked inside a room. I want to ask everyone to leave it the hell alone, but I worry that if I even mention it, someone will break open the door and gape at my pain without my permission. Or shame me as "unhealthy" because I won't lock myself inside that room and watch myself get hurt over and over. Or torture me with the same thoughts I use to torture myself.

Or.

Or.

Or.

I deserve to have the key to my own

memories, my own trauma. I deserve to decide when and with whom I share that trauma. I deserve the right to move on — or not.

I deserve what my rapist never gave me: a choice.

CRUDE COLLAGES OF MY MOTHER

I haven't seen my mother in more than five years. I haven't seen her the way I choose to remember her for much longer. Her unmatched energy, her unabashed goofiness, her unvarnished love. And her smile. It's been a long time since I've seen that.

I could never objectively assess her beauty. Her personality eclipsed her features — one of those rare people who is somehow above menial things like physical appearance. She radiated outward. In my mind she is forever tinged by orange light — a sunset, perhaps, or an open flame. The further I get from that person, that vision, the more I try to write her into existence — a literary séance I hope will inch closer to catharsis. But words haven't alleviated my guilt, and words definitely haven't helped her navigate the systems that have shoved her and held her down. It's that part of her life which I labour to forget, to my nausea and shame.

My mother has bipolar disorder. I have never liked the starkness of that word, "bipolar." In three syllables it eschews all nuance and subtlety. A word so strong even I tend to think of her in terms of her position between these two theoretical "poles" instead of as a living, breathing human with a range of emotions. Is she depressed this time, or manic? Sleeping too much, or not enough? In every conversation we have, I attempt to dictate her mental health, or rewrite her history, or diagnose her emotions until they're mere clinical terms. After all, I'm the sane one.

My mother has so many odd facets of her life and personality that piecing everything together is like viewing a Tom Wesselmann collage: there is a surprised satisfaction in recognizing the disparate parts, a strange contentment in realizing such different parts form such a complete work, then finally an unsettling sense of wrongness once one considers how contradictory those parts are. If I were to make a list of descriptors that could define my mother in order of what I consider to be most important to her, it would look like this:

1. Mother of eight

2. White (ex)wife to Mohawk man (Race supposedly not important to her, but important nonetheless.)
3. Fervent Catholic (Could explain 1.)
4. Computer genius (Offered a job by NASA, turned down so my older sister with cerebral palsy could stay at the facility she was in.)
5. Kung fu master (Sixth-degree black belt, to be exact.)

I could add other things, like her star athleticism and resultant eating disorder in high school, or her contradictory food bingeing and weight gain in married life, or the history of mental illness in her family (her closest brother committed suicide; her youngest brother struggled with addiction for over twenty years; her mother dealt with dementia; I suspect her father had schizophrenia or bipolar disorder, since he was prescribed lithium, but there's no one left who will tell me). I could bring up the isolation she felt being dragged from America to the Six Nations reserve in Canada without any legal protection or permission. All of those are only parts.

The last time I saw her sick (again those poles! As if she could be simply classified as merely "sick" or "healthy") she was homeless and had just gotten out of jail. My dad had had her arrested for stabbing a holiday cookie tin and leaving it on the porch or, as the courts called it, "threats" and "domestic abuse." A restraining order and a week in jail later, she was out on bail and visiting me at work. She approached the lottery kiosk I was working at narrow-eyed, headband pulled across her head the way women did in the early '90s. Her personal style was like a testament to the time before my dad, a time capsule she couldn't bury. I could see the illness starting to work its way under her skin, transforming her. Her entire face looked different when she was manic. Her pupils were giant, surrounded by only small circles of green. Her lips were curled in a grimace, wrinkles like parentheses around her mouth, crescents of blue-tinged skin drooping below her eyes. And her jaw always set as if she were waiting for a fight.

Within a week of her release my mom went missing. My sister and I found her charging down the street in downtown Brantford, her lips moving fast as she yelled at no one and everyone. We managed to get her back to my place. Pacing, shaking, eyeballs darting, muscles tensing. I'll never forget the way she looked at the TV in my living room as she told me someone was listening to us from inside it. There was unshakable confidence in that look.

I'm not sure what she remembers of all this, if she remembers anything. She could argue with surprising credibility that nothing was wrong with her at all, that she just had post-traumatic stress disorder. She'd say it calmly and coolly, as if post-traumatic stress was something a person agreed to during a marriage ceremony with a decisive "I do." But then I'd mention things she'd rather forget. The time she tried to rip our thirty-two-inch TV from the wall because it was evil. The time she trashed our house with the destructive artistry of an entitled rock star. The time she thought demons were in our trailer. She threw a knife at the couch right next to me in an attempt to "kill them." If I bring this up with her, she tells me that she didn't think there were demons at all; she was just really angry; I'm making it all up. I wonder whether she really believes that or if it's something she has to believe.

Recently I've read about people with bipolar disorder experiencing memory loss. One person, a computer programmer like my mother, was unable to keep his job because things he knew before he got sick apparently flew to the farthest recesses of his mind once bipolar disorder set in. The theory is that the bipolar person is too stimulated when manic to focus on what's happening around them, making it difficult to create new memories. When depressed, the person feels too bad about themselves to see anything but their perceived flaws, thus nothing is remembered but the feeling of worthlessness. But what about good old-fashioned repression? What of not wanting to remember the things you did when you were on sensory overload, or the people who had to tend to you when you were so depressed you couldn't bathe yourself? Who would want to remember their kids' muffled cries from another room, their small bodies tense and taut as violin strings?

Most of the time when we talk, my mother and I just pretend nothing ever happened, though the evidence of it is always there. Everything we say to one another bears the weight of our unacknowledged, ever-present, fucked-up family history. I can't look at her or talk to her without feeling it, darting in and out of my mind's peripherals like some thick-limbed jungle cat. There's only so much a person can repress.

Ironically, it has always helped me to split my mom in two: Normal Mom and Bipolar Mom. Whenever I have to interact with Bipolar Mom, I seem to entirely forget

Normal Mom, the mom I love, who knew my schoolgirl crushes and laughed at every one of my terrible jokes and pushed aside her steadfast religion to help me through my teenage pregnancy. I think of Bipolar Mom as something entirely other, a beast so terrible that it doesn't deserve the courtesy of courtesy. I wonder if my mother thinks the same thing of herself, if she compartmentalizes things she has done and labels them "Under the Influence of Bipolar" or "Entirely Mine." Maybe she doesn't think about these things at all. Maybe she can't.

Kanye West revealed he was diagnosed with bipolar disorder on his 2018 album, "Ye." Across the cover, over a moody image of mountains and swirling clouds, are the words:

I hate being
Bi-Polar
its awesome

I wasn't surprised. I've always analyzed the erratic behaviour of others, mentally checking off symptoms before confidently, quietly announcing to my husband, "That person reminds me of my mom. They probably have bipolar disorder." I said this about Britney Spears in 2007, when now-infamous photos emerged of her swinging a green umbrella at a photographer — her head freshly shaved, her eyes dark pits that looked but didn't seem to see. I said this about a complete stranger on the streets of Toronto asking for change who, when I gave him some of my change but not all of it, started following me, spitting insults with an anger that vibrated on another frequency. I said this about Kanye when I saw him perform live in 2013. Three-quarters of the way through his incredible two-hour-long set he gave a rambling fifteen-minute speech that started with a declaration that, despite portrayals to the contrary, he wasn't angry at all, that he was "extremely happy." As his words tumbled out and tangled up, Kanye never worried whether we were following his logic. He didn't seem to care. "If I say something completely stupid, completely fucked, it don't matter," he said. "If I say something that's completely inspiring . . . take that with you, apply that to your life." He spoke with the focus and confidence of a motivational speaker. He spoke until he felt like stopping.

I saw all of these symptoms when my mother was manic: the eyes of Britney, the anger of the stranger, the conviction of Kanye. When she was manic she would talk for hours, usually about my father and all the fucked-up things he'd done to her. She'd talk until her throat was raw and her voice rasping. She'd talk even if it was two in the morning and the person she was talking at was trying to sleep. It didn't faze her. After all, she wasn't having a conversation, not really. She was delivering a sermon. We kids were supposed to nod at her accusations and revelations like true believers at church, affirming everything she said as though hers was the very voice of God. If she asked a yes or no question, her gaze fiery and fixed and waiting for our response, and we gave the wrong answer, her voice would become louder, sharper. "Oh, you don't think he's irresponsible? Do you have any idea how much money he owes your grandmother? Do you know what he did with that money?" We could either continue to question her account of our father, ensuring we were screamed at for hours, or we could ridicule him, too, hoping that with Mom's aim trained back on its original target, we could slink away, unnoticed.

This was life with Mom's mania: the anger, the yelling, the way she'd keep us all up, even on school nights, because the entire world needed to know what was on her mind. Aunts, uncles, cousins, cashiers, neighbours, priests, teachers, police officers — all of them would hear her. God himself would hear her. She made sure of it.

All the while I felt like I was being swallowed by quicksand. I had to make sure my younger siblings had dinner, that the food didn't erupt in flames because Mom left it unattended to send dozens of emails to strangers in Sweden about investing in her computer business. I had to argue with my mother when she decided *Resident Evil* — the game we played together as a family for years — was demonic and needed to be removed from the house so our family could heal. I had to go to school every day and pretend that I was happy and whole and got more than three hours of sleep.

Unlike our father, I couldn't just drive off and stay away until eleven at night, pretending Mom didn't exist. As soon as I got home from school, I had to endure every minute of her illness along with her. I have no idea where my father went all those hours, all those days. He didn't have a job half the time, he didn't volunteer anywhere, he didn't bring home friends. All I knew was he was gone and we were alone and I hated him for it. I hated my mother, too — for scaring Dad away, for staying with him, for reminding me that a calm house was a privilege.

I hated her being bipolar most of all.

Just before Mom's brain was firing too fast to let her sleep, before her repressed anger could boil over and burn everyone around her, there was a period that all of us loved. We loved it so much we refused to admit it was connected to her bipolar disorder. For the days or weeks she inhabited that liminal space it was as though she had complete control of the best parts of her personality. She was charming, funny, excited. A current of electricity ran through her, lighting her eyes and words. When she was like this we couldn't help ourselves; we twisted ourselves over and around one another like weeds to capture the warmth of her full attention. We'd gather around, waiting for her to do a goofy dance, or buy a tub of ice cream so we could make sundaes, or watch the *Mortal Kombat* movie with us again, leaping up to show us kung fu during the fight scenes. She was more fun than any other mom we'd ever known.

Six months from now, she'd say, we're going to be rich, and then she'd buy us everything we'd ever wanted: art supplies, a canopy bed, a whole new wardrobe, a mansion with an indoor swimming pool and big-screen TVs in every room, a Jacuzzi hot tub, a complete set of holographic Pokémon cards. Even our dad couldn't resist the fairy tale. He'd listen, rapt, as she laid out the latest business plan or pyramid scheme she was sure would get us rich quick. All it would cost is an initial investment of $299.99, which we'd make back within a month. She'd sit at the computer, her fingers tapping out possibilities on the keyboard, her eyes darting, searching for the best opportunity a banner ad could sell. She'd stay up late, get up early, her face constantly awash in the blue glow of the monitor. Then she'd become obsessed, easily irritated, her laughter skittering to a stop and her jokes morphing to sharp chastisements whenever we interrupted her. That was about the time the fun part of her mania seamlessly transformed into the difficult part.

Just before that, though, if you were to tell us that the excitement and energy we loved so much were part of Mom's mania, that her hard work and hustle were at their height when she was manic, that she was at her most hilarious, fun and focused then, we'd probably say her bipolar was awesome, too. It was always awesome until it wasn't.

As a child, and even as a teen, when my father told me the signs that my mother's mental health was deteriorating, I believed him. I believed that identifying these signs, collecting them like baseball cards, and shoving them before her face to stare at when she was at her most argumentative — or most depressed — was being a good partner. I believed that forcing her into a car, turning on the child locks so she couldn't jump out and shuttling her over the border, where New York laws would allow her to be involuntarily admitted to the mental hospital, was the only way to support a mentally ill person.

I began to question these assumptions when I grew up, primarily because I became the partner of a person with severe clinical depression. Mike had a rough time with his depression in university and barely finished his classes. He would cry in bed almost every day the last year of school, saying awful, untrue things about himself, often wanting to hurt himself, even kill himself. I had no idea what to do. My experience with my mother hadn't prepared me for this. I only knew how my father would approach the situation: forced hospitalization and medication. But I also remembered how traumatized my mother was by those hospitalizations; I remembered when she couldn't recall simple words because her medication interfered with her brain too badly, how she'd eventually erupt in frustrated tears. I didn't want those things for Mike. I didn't want them for her, either. Instead of getting cops or doctors involved, I tried to talk Mike through his depression, countering the negative self-talk in his head with all the evidence his depressed brain wouldn't let him see. *You're not a bad person. You're not a burden. You are not your depression.* I looked up how to talk to suicidal people, learned the crucial difference between passive thoughts of dying, thoughts of suicide and active plans for suicide. Somehow, despite my fumbled attempts to support him, Mike managed to pull himself out of the depression — and somehow I managed to convince myself that his depression was a one-time thing.

When it came back every year or so over the next ten years, it would hit with the force of a fighter jet. I tried to find ways to help. I read books about supporting depressed partners. I persuaded Mike to go to a therapist. I supported him when he and the therapist decided their four sessions were all he needed. I convinced him to go on medication. I supported him when he insisted on taking himself off medication to save our family money. I didn't always agree with his decisions, but they were his decisions to make. I didn't want him to feel as though my opinions on his treatment mattered more than his, the way my father had with my mother. I kept wondering what would have happened if my dad had talked to my mom about her experiences, consulted with her about her treatment, let her have some autonomy over what happened to her body and mind. Would she have accepted that she had bipolar disorder years ago? Gone through the long, gruelling process of figuring out a treatment plan and support system that allowed her to have a more stable life? Or would everything be exactly the same, with Mom still struggling to admit her diagnosis today?

Here's the thing: despite criticizing my mother for not admitting her mental illness, and despite assuring my husband that depression was nothing to be ashamed of, it took me until I was twenty-six to admit that I had severe depression and anxiety. I didn't want to admit that the creeping ivy of my mother's genetics had taken hold in my

214

mind, climbing its walls, obscuring every good part of my life. I saw the way Mom was treated by police, doctors, nurses, cashiers, total strangers and family members. They could all tell that there was something different about her; they would look at her with a mixture of fear and revulsion, as if she were a rabid dog. I didn't want to be looked at and dehumanized that way. I was terrified that if I admitted my problems to myself, every person who thought of me as strong, put-together and fearless would see my mental illness peeking out from behind my eyes and turn on me, the way everyone had eventually turned on my mom. History would repeat itself through me.

I had always asked Mom, *Why can't you admit there's something wrong with you?* Now I knew. With Mike's unending love and support, I eventually admitted my mental health issues. Still, it took another four years for me to work up the nerve to ask my doctor for medication, and another six months after that for me to realize that I should probably take it every day as prescribed. There was another question I'd always asked Mom: *Why can't you just take your meds?* I knew that now, too.

Just before I decided to go back on my medication, I cried every day. *You're not a bad person. You're not a burden. You are not your depression,* I told myself, repeating the words I used to say to Mike until they tasted like ash on my tongue. I didn't believe any of them. I couldn't. The depression made that impossible.

It's easy to tell a person who has a physical illness that they are not their cold, or their diabetes, or their stroke. Their illness is something that happens to them, affects their life — sometimes in incredibly difficult ways — but it still isn't *them.* It's harder to make that distinction when you have a mental illness that completely changes the way you express your personality, the way you interact with others, the way you see the world. Where do you end and where does your sickness begin?

When I was at a writing residency a few years ago, I read from a piece that took my experience of depression and heavily fictionalized it, turning the worst experience of my life into what I hoped was art. One of the mentors of the program approached me afterwards, expressing how much she could relate to the narrator's hatred of her good, loving husband because she'd felt the same way about a really great person she'd once dated. I explained to her that wasn't what was going on, that my narrator didn't hate her husband at all, that her undiagnosed depression was convincing her that she did. The mentor gave me a blank look and claimed she didn't understand. I tried again, telling her the narrator's emotions were based on how I felt about myself when I was depressed. I would dwell on everything wrong with me, telling myself that I was unlovable, that I was better off dead. But I didn't actually feel that way most of the time. Depression had slid over my eyes like a lens, tinting everything I saw, thought and experienced until I no longer remembered what life was like before.

"I still don't get it. How do you know what's you and what's the depression?"

Nothing I said would make her understand. She clearly hadn't experienced the sort of depression I had, so anything I said would be theoretical to her, a thought exercise instead of a devastating, ongoing lived experience. Often, deep in my sickness, I'd wonder whether depression was my natural state. Maybe there was no point to anything, and all the things I could possibly do or experience were just a series of shallow attempts to distract myself from the bottomless void of life. That very well could be true, but having known the depths of depression intimately meant that I would no longer be tactless enough to ask a person with mental health issues a question like that. It meant I would have empathy for others with depression, that I wouldn't call those who lost their battle with depression "cowards" or "selfish" or "assholes" for committing suicide. It also meant I would appreciate being healthy much more than if I'd never been depressed.

"You don't know what's you and what's the depression when you're still depressed," I finally answered. "That's why it sucks so much."

X-Men character Jean Grey has an evil alter ego named Dark Phoenix. Dark Phoenix is unbridled power, a god that cares for nothing and no one, being channelled through the compassionate, heroic Jean Grey. Once she is Jean Grey again, and has to deal with the consequences of her actions as Dark Phoenix, she is grief-ridden. Her friends try to tell her it wasn't her who did those things, it was the Phoenix, but Jean Grey realizes that even though she and Phoenix are separate, they're bound together. One cannot exist without the other, and so long as Jean Grey lives, Dark Phoenix will eventually manifest. Eventually Jean Grey volunteers to be killed so Dark Phoenix can never take control of her again.

It seems to me my mother is often at the mercy of her sickness, waiting for her own Dark Phoenix to take hold. So is Mike. So am I. And though I try to mentally split my mother in two, to make her "Normal" or "Bipolar," she isn't. She deserves a fuller range of adjectives and acknowledgements than that. I may not understand her with the conviction I feel I understand a good literary character, or have perfect bouquets of flowery memories unmarred by pain, but I do think I know her. Distance may make the picture fuzzy, but it always does. Crude collaging may, indeed, be the only way to reassemble her person and our past. But really, is that any different than what we do with anyone? Sculpt people into the archetypes we prefer to imagine instead of the people they are? Isn't that why it offends us so much when those we love do something that makes no sense to us, even when to them it's an obvious and perhaps inevitable choice?

It's hard to let go of control, to stop trying to be the architect of not only our own lives but the lives of the people around us as we single-mindedly work towards our own flawed constructions of "perfection." Once we do, though, we might actually be able to recognize the beauty we've missed. Witness the glimpses of unplanned perfection that have been there all along, perhaps hidden in the few rushed lines of a Facebook message, or in an unasked-for Catechism bought and mailed after months of scrimping and saving, or in the eyes of a mother whose life may have never been easy but whose love has always, always prevailed, ensuring her daughter would prevail, too.

SONTAG, IN SNAPSHOTS
REFLECTING ON
"IN PLATO'S CAVE" IN 2018

"In teaching us a new visual code,
photographs alter and enlarge our notions
of what is worth looking at and what we
have a right to observe. They are . . . an
ethics of seeing."
— SUSAN SONTAG, "IN PLATO'S CAVE"

I started to dodge cameras around the age
of ten. Photos, I thought, were meant to
preserve images of the beautiful. I was not
beautiful. I was ugly, and therefore not
worth being immortalized on film or —
more recently — in digital images. Any time
I saw myself in a photo at one specific moment, at one specific angle, I felt sick. *Why
did they take that picture?* I'd wonder. Who
would want to look at an ugly girl like me? I
didn't even want to look at me.

Despite my tendency to avoid pictures,
when I was eighteen I realized the more I
tried to avoid being photographed, the more

people tried to photograph me. It was like a game to them. It didn't matter that I didn't like being photographed. It didn't matter that they were my friends. They were going to get a picture of me. They were going to prove to me that getting my picture taken wasn't so bad. These people would eventually get their picture, but they never proved anything to me about photos. All they proved to me was that their desire to have an image of me was more important to them than what I wanted. This was their ethics of seeing me. I had no power over it.

I stopped resisting photos after that. I wouldn't pose, I wouldn't smile. I'd make an intentionally ugly face in a half-hearted attempt to get the jump on people who might criticize my unintentionally ugly face. I'd make an intentionally ugly face to stop myself from criticizing what I thought of as my unintentionally ugly face.

"[Photographs] give us the sense that we can hold the whole world in our heads. . . . To collect photographs is to collect the world."

The idea of "owning" the world is hardly new. In fact, the desire to own or collect the world is behind the colonialism that has

222

overtaken every corner of this planet. Photography itself has had an interesting role in colonialism, one that can be traced back to famous painter George Catlin. The story goes that in 1805, when he was nine, Catlin encountered an Oneida man from the Haudenosaunee Confederacy. This man didn't kill, kidnap or harm Catlin, which were all things that "savage Indians" were apparently supposed to do back then. The man simply raised his hand in acknowledgement.

This act was enough to shatter the stereotype Catlin had grown up believing. Unfortunately, Catlin took that knowledge and invested his energies into memorializing another stereotype: that of the vanishing Indian. Catlin believed that it was inevitable that Indigenous peoples would die out — either from illnesses like smallpox or from war. Instead of petitioning his government to stop slaughtering us, though, Catlin resigned himself to our extinction and took it upon himself to preserve "the looks and customs of the vanishing races of native man in America." He even wrote, "Nothing short of the loss of my life, shall prevent me from visiting their country, and of becoming their historian." Not even Indigenous peoples' consent, it would seem.

Despite his presumably friendly intentions, Catlin painted without knowing what ceremonies he was observing or concerning himself with how those he painted felt about his work. The paintings he created were his truth, but they were presented as if they were *the* truth.

A little over a hundred years after Catlin's life-changing encounter with a Haudenosaunee man, Edward S. Curtis published the first volume in his *The North American Indian* project. Like Catlin before him, Curtis travelled to different Indigenous nations for his project — but unlike Catlin, Curtis used photography to capture his versions of "an Indian character . . . [at] some vital phase in his existence." Curtis produced thousands of photos and twenty volumes of those photos. But when I look at those photos, I don't see the person the way I think they want to be seen. I see them the way Curtis wanted them to be seen: frozen in time, relics of the past, beautifully tragic vanishing Indians.

The (white, often male) idea that preserving Indigenous peoples' images is somehow more important than us preserving our own traditions and lives is just as intoxicating for non-Indigenous people today as it was in Catlin's day. In 2013, British photographer

Jimmy Nelson published his series "Before They Pass Away," which — you guessed it — is another attempt by a white man to deem himself the official historian of nations he does not know, and to preserve specific, staged images of the people within them. Writer and photographer Teju Cole writes that Nelson "is sentimental about those he photographs and often proclaims their beauty, but having invested himself so deeply in the idea of their 'disappearance,' he is unable to believe that they are not going anywhere, that they are simply adapting to the modern world." How many non-Indigenous people are just as deeply invested as Nelson and Curtis and Catlin in the idea that we are vanishing Indians? How many have looked at these men's images of us, thought that we were beautiful, bought photos or paintings of us, collected those images, but never once spoken to any of us in person? Never once considered what our lives today are like, or how they personally contribute to our ongoing dispossession and disappearance?

This "beauty" of ours that they claim to admire rarely translates to their seeing us in our fullness — as unique, sovereign peoples who deserve the right to control our own destinies. It does nothing to advance our rights or interests because, quite simply, these people don't see human beings. They see an ideology, an aesthetic; a story that reinforces their self-proclaimed right to occupy Indigenous lands without making them feel bad for how they got that "right." If they were to see us as anything more than an aesthetic, they would have to acknowledge their own complicity in upholding the exact systems that have been trying to disappear us for centuries.

In 2015 I was at a writing residency for emerging Indigenous writers at a national arts institution. When they were looking to photograph a few of the participants to feature on their website, I knew they wouldn't choose me. I didn't look like the vanishing Indians Nelson, Curtis and Catlin loved so much. I didn't look Indian© at all. Sure enough, they picked writers with long black hair and high cheekbones and beautiful, tawny skin. They knew exactly what they were looking for to get the visual diversity points they so clearly craved. The writers they chose didn't have their traditional regalia with them for the pictures, but I can only imagine the boundless enthusiasm the literary officer of the program would have had if they did. They could have collected their perfect Indian© image to add to their collection, an image they knew to look for because of Nelson, Curtis and Catlin.

"Photographs furnish evidence. . . .
The camera record incriminates."

When Black Lives Matter started mobilizing around police violence against Black people in the wake of the murders of Eric Garner and Michael Brown, many people thought that the solution was body cameras. If photographs furnish evidence, went their logic, surely camera footage could furnish all the evidence needed to prove, or disprove, charges of racist police violence. Of course many Black people, Indigenous people and people of colour suspected that this wouldn't be the case, but white people — people who had never had reason to fear police — were adamant.

There are instances where anti-Black police violence caught on film has been used as evidence. Twenty-seven-year-old Philip Alafe was taken into the Brantford police station on July 3, 2015, after an arrest. He told the booking officer he had depression and anxiety, though he wasn't suicidal, and that he had sickle cell anemia, thus requiring regular medication to help alleviate his ongoing pain. Alafe is, it's important to note, a Black man.

Staff Sergeant Cheney Venn, a white police officer, came on duty at 10:30 p.m. (I feel obliged to disclose that Venn was the police officer at my high school when I went there from 2002 until 2006, though I never interacted with him personally.) Alafe, hoping for more medication, began throwing wet toilet paper at the camera around 11 p.m. to get the attention of the officers on duty. Venn yelled at him to stop. When Alafe wouldn't stop, Venn removed Alafe's mattress and blanket from his cell, telling him he'd get them back when he behaved. He gave Alafe one pill, though Alafe was allowed up to three if needed. Still in pain, and wanting his mattress and blanket back, Alafe tied his jumpsuit and shirt to the bars of his cell over the next few hours. Venn came back twice and told him not to do that. He didn't return his mattress or blanket.

At 3 a.m., Venn came back to Alafe's cell and punched him three times, then he took his jumpsuit and all other clothing from him except for his socks, leaving him naked and cold in his cell. (Alafe's doctor has described his pain as "unbearable" — and, unfortunately, made even worse by cold, dehydra-

228

tion and stress.) Meanwhile, Venn, who admitted in court he hadn't tried to determine what Alafe's medical conditions were, decided Alafe did not need medical attention or more medication. He thought Alafe's claiming to have a chronic condition was simply an attempt "to get out of the cells in order to go to a more comfortable setting."

After Alafe spent three hours in pain, shivering naked on the floor, his depression got the better of him and he tried to fashion a noose out of his socks. It took two minutes for Venn to stop Alafe's suicide attempt, after which he took his socks and still refused to get him medical attention.

At 7:30 a.m., when a new officer took over from Venn, he returned Alafe's jumpsuit and, shortly after, his mattress and blanket. Unsurprisingly, once Alafe finally had clothes, a blanket and a mattress, he fell asleep.

The reason I can relay all of this in detail — and the reason Ontario Court Justice Ken Lenz stayed the charges against Alafe, finding Alafe's rights were violated under sections 7 and 12 of the Charter of Rights and Freedoms — is because the incident was caught on camera. Justice Lenz admitted that without the cell videos he probably would have believed Officer Venn's version of events. He needed proof. He needed the camera record.

And yet even though Lenz thoroughly rebuked Venn's behaviour, calling it "degrading to human dignity," and claimed that Alafe's perception that he could no longer trust police was "a perception I'm beginning to share," Venn, his abuser, remained on regular duty as a police officer. Brantford police chief Geoffrey Nelson has said there is an ongoing investigation into "potential professional misconduct," but there is no guarantee that Venn's abusing a Black, disabled man will cost him his job, or even lead to a few weeks of paid leave. After all, the officers who killed Eric Garner on camera were not indicted. The officer who shot Philando Castile while his girlfriend, Diamond Reynolds, live-streamed the encounter to Facebook was not indicted. The officer who shot twelve-year-old Tamir Rice on camera was not indicted. So few of the white police officers who beat or kill Black people are ever indicted, or even punished.

The systems responsible for creating an environment where Officer Venn could abuse Alafe without worrying about the consequences, the systems that created Alafe's story in the first place, continue — unchanged and unchecked. No matter how incriminating certain photos may be, and no matter how much people who have never experienced anti-Black racism claim otherwise, there is no photographic record that can change these systems. Not on its own.

"In deciding how a picture should look, in preferring one exposure to another, photographers are always imposing standards on their subjects."

The agency of photographers and lack of agency of their subjects often gets overlooked, mainly because photographs are usually seen as facts rather than crafted images. It's assumed that photography, and therefore photographers, are passive, merely showing the world as it is. Sontag refers to the passive nature of photography as "its aggression," arguing that even idealizing subjects or making a "virtue of [their] plainness" is an aggressive act. The popularity of certain types of photographs of poor folk, racialized folk, disabled folk and so on would seem to argue against the charge of aggression — at first. I'm thinking of the work of people like Diane Arbus, who photographed "freaks," or Jacob Riis, who photographed the poor, or Adam Clark Vroman, who photographed Indigenous people, or perhaps even Robert Mapplethorpe, who photographed naked Black men for his *Black Book.* Aren't these photographs trying to educate those of us who don't have access to those people, those spaces? Aren't they trying to encourage understanding, education, empathy?

Perhaps. But how can understanding, education, or empathy exist when all you have is the photograph? When you have no context to educate you on what, exactly, you're seeing and what, exactly, it means? Without that, viewers must rely on their own assumptions and their own often limited knowledge. If you're looking at a photo in *National Geographic,* for instance, and you see an "exotic" African man from an unspecified tribe, you have the illusion of being educated. You now know that that person, that way of living, exists. But you don't know what his clothing or tattoos or facial piercings mean to him or his people, what his people have survived, what they care about or who they are. You know only what that person looked like at that exact second, in that exact light.

So how, then, is the photo operating? Is it telling you what that man wants you to know, or is it allowing you to act as a voyeur, smuggling you into his space without his consent — a space you wouldn't otherwise have access to? Is it giving you the option of looking at this man from a "safe distance," maybe curled up on your couch, or sitting in the waiting room of your dental office, all the while not giving the man you're looking at the opportunity to speak back to you or correct your assumptions about him?

This may be why, in March 2018, *National Geographic*'s newest editor-in-chief, Susan Goldberg, penned an editorial about the magazine's historical depiction of race. I could go into detail about Goldberg's arguments and examples, but the title really says it all: "For Decades, Our Coverage Was Racist. To Rise Above Our Past, We Must Acknowledge It." The most telling part of the article was when John Edwin Mason, who teaches the history of photography at the University of Virginia, pointed out that *National Geographic* came "into existence at the height of colonialism, [when] the world was divided into the colonizers and the colonized." Mason argued that the magazine didn't teach so much as reinforce ideas readers already had, while giving them photographic "proof" that these racist ideas were, in fact, correct. This has always been the danger of not taking into consideration who the photographer is and what standards they are trying to impose.

This is also why there seems to be such a stark contrast between the types of photos taken by photographers who have no understanding of who or what they're photographing and photos taken by photographers who do. In her photo series "Concrete Indians," Anishinaabe/Ojibway photographer Nadya Kwandibens, from the Animakee Wa Zhing First Nation, asks, "Who are you as a Native person living in the city?" Kwandibens contrasts her subjects — Indigenous people wearing their traditional regalia or "modern" clothes or some combination of the two — with the heavily urban, concrete spaces around them. If that juxtaposition feels unusual or wrong to you, her photos seem to say, that's not our problem. That's *your* problem. Do you think Indigenous people are relics? That they don't belong in cities? Do you think they should only be wearing "modern" clothing in these spaces? Do you think they should just assimilate already?

2Spirit/Queer Métis/Saulteaux/Polish visual artist Dayna Danger uses BDSM, beaded fetish masks and the strategic placement of antlers in huge-scale photos that, in Danger's own words, question "the line between empowerment and objectification"

234

and explore "the complicated dynamics of sexuality, gender, and power in a consensual and feminist manner." Her photos demand your attention, demand you look in the eyes of the Black or Indigenous woman you might otherwise dismiss or demean and see the power of choice. She is choosing to show you her body, to show you her desire, to look you in the eye, to not be ashamed. That is the pinnacle of decolonization: an empowered, unashamed Black woman beside an empowered, unashamed Indigenous woman.

British artist Alison Lapper, who was born without arms and with shortened legs, a condition called phocomelia, turns her photographic eye on herself, interrogating ideas of beauty and physical normality in pictures that are sometimes bold and sexy, sometimes soft and sensual. The very idea that a disabled woman is worthy of the sort of love and attention art requires is radical; the idea that she can make that art herself is revolutionary. Lapper's work questions the notion that disabled people are objects to pity or use for inspiration. Instead of seeing them as "sad" or "inspirational," see them as sexual, see them as beautiful, see them as human.

There are many photographers who have

used cameras to craft images of their own communities on their own terms. These photographers are intimately aware of how the wrong people imposing the wrong standards can push harmful narratives about their communities — narratives that can result in real-life negative repercussions for their family and friends. These photographers have a stake in accurately representing their communities, so with every photograph they take, they're aware of the responsibility they carry. After all, if they do a bad job portraying their own communities, they'll have to clean up the mess, too.

However, when a person enters another community as a tourist, bringing their own set of unexamined, perhaps problematic assumptions with them, they're not necessarily going to be held accountable for how their photographs uphold those assumptions. No matter how long they're in that space taking pictures, they're going to leave when they're done. They don't have to look any of their subjects in the eye and explain to them why they removed certain things from the image and added others. They don't have to deal with any negative repercussions that could arise as a result of their inaccuracies. The most they have to confront is the possibility that their photographic subjects will later contact them and express discontent with their work. Since it's still ultimately the photographer's choice whether to listen to the critique and make changes, that's not exactly a heavy burden to bear.

I don't believe you necessarily have to be part of a community to take their concerns about representation seriously. Aaron Huey is a white photographer living in Seattle. When he went to photograph the Oglala Lakota tribe on the Pine Ridge Reservation in South Dakota back in 2005, he was looking to photograph poverty in America. That was the standard he was imposing on his subjects. It didn't take long for him to realize the flaw with his approach. "People there were telling me the most epic stories I'd ever heard," Huey told *Slate,* "and people were talking about a history of genocide. I knew that word would never be used in the mainstream press. I knew right away I wasn't OK with that, that I wanted a bigger piece of the truth than just more statistics and more pictures of poverty."

Huey spent four years at Pine Ridge, becoming part of the community, falling in love with the families that invited him in. Even though what he saw on that reserve was "the saddest and scariest thing I'd seen on the face of the Earth," he knew that "objective" journalism wasn't the right way to approach this. He had to learn the history of oppression he represented as a white man, as well as protocols for ceremonies he didn't understand. For example, he learned he was allowed to photograph before and after ceremonies, but not during. The Lakota people themselves also challenged his intentions: according to a *Time* article, "When they thought he wasn't capturing the reality of it all, they'd say: 'Why are you doing this?' He would ask himself 'Why *am* I doing this?' and recalibrate." It took every one of those four years before he felt he had "learned how to hear [the Lakota people]," and moved from a passive observer to an actual advocate, collaborating on street art projects, storytelling projects, non-profit work that funds Indigenous artists, and a cover story with none other than *National Geographic.*

When Huey published *Mitakuye Oyasin,* a book of his photography of Pine Ridge, he had spent over seven years there. He described the book as "more like a prayer or a poem than a documentary. It was like a ceremony, and I didn't realize it until the end." Through his experience with the Lakota people, Huey realized how unsatisfying it was acting as an "impartial witness" to the events he was photographing, and subsequently changed his entire approach to photography. In order to understand and honour his responsibility to the Lakota community, Huey had to acknowledge and take accountability for the shallow standards he wanted to impose, and choose to impose entirely different ones instead.

When you look at the photos of Nadya Kwandibens, Dayna Danger, Alison Lapper and Aaron Huey, you can feel the respect that has shaped each frame. It's a completely different viewing experience. Each photographer respected and understood the communities they were photographing before they snapped their shutter closed. They knew their photos bore a responsibility, so their work was created with more care and intention than if they worked under the colonial assumption that they had the "right" to photograph whatever they wanted, however they wanted. The bare minimum we should expect photographers to impose on their subjects is respect.

"From its start, photography implied the capture of the largest possible number of subjects. Painting never had so imperial a scope."

The magnitude of photography, the way it aims to capture everything, does indeed seem to have an imperial scope. It's even more pervasive now than when Sontag wrote her book. Technology has absolutely infiltrated our lives with cameras, allowing us every opportunity to take thousands of pictures of ourselves and others whenever the desire strikes. Sontag claimed back in 1973 that photography's popularity meant it was "not practiced by most people as art," but one has only to look at the popularity of Instagram, photo-editing apps and cell phones with high-quality cameras to see that this assertion holds little weight today. People not only want to take pictures of their everyday lives; they want to craft and manipulate them until they look like they were taken by professionals.

The term "selfie" was coined by an Australian man in 2002, yet perhaps unsurprisingly the cultural stigma surrounding selfies seems proportional to how popular they are with women. It's an interesting bit of bullshit: Women can be the subject of millions of paintings hung in galleries, often painted by men. Women can be in varying states of undress in photos used for advertisements, often photographed by men. Women can appear in films, TV shows, fashion spreads, porn — often shot, directed and edited by men. Women's bodies can be posed and prodded and digitally manipulated until they look nothing like the real women who stood in front of the camera. That's all fine. But if a woman puts on makeup, takes a picture of herself, for herself, adds a filter or two and posts it on Instagram, men comment that this is why you can't trust women, that women are engaging in "false advertising," that all men should take women swimming on the first date to see how they *really* look under all the makeup and photoshop.

Of course, it's not just men who hate women who post selfies. I used to be a selfie-hater, too. I would scroll through social media, resentment and indignation welling in my chest as picture after picture of smiling women or sexy women or serious women or goofy women came up on my screen. I was always the most annoyed at women who were trying to look sexy or beautiful in their selfies. *What narcissists,* I thought, choking down my own insecurity.

It was only when I decided I didn't have to see myself as ugly that I actively interrogated this impulse. Why was I tearing down these women — many of whom were my coworkers, my acquaintances, my friends? What was so wrong with them feeling good about the way they looked? For exerting control over their own image in a world that insisted control should never belong to them? For getting validation that they were, in the words of Rachel Syme, "worthy of being seen"?

I started taking photos of myself. It *did* make me feel beautiful. It *did* make me see myself as worthy of being seen. But I still wouldn't share my selfies with anyone else. In her brilliant essay "Selfie: The Revolutionary Potential of Your Own Face, in Seven Chapters," Rachel Syme defines a selfie as having to be shared in order to be considered a selfie. I balked at this initially. Weren't my selfies selfies? Why did I have to share pictures of myself when I was taking them solely for my own satisfaction?

Then I remembered the shame, the ugliness that I felt back when I was a kid who refused to have my picture taken. How I was convinced no one would want to see a picture of me. How I hated seeing pictures of myself. Even though I was almost two decades older and had embarked on a project to see myself as beautiful, very little had changed. I still thought keeping pictures of myself from others was, in a sense, sparing them.

If photography has a scope we could call "imperial," what would we call the scope of something as ingrained and unavoidable as shame? Perhaps we should also call it "imperial." After all, haven't the Western, white-centric beauty standards that have made us feel inadequate and shameful in the first place been spread through imperialism? Though Britain can no longer claim most of the world as its empire, the colonialism it introduced — the beauty standards it introduced — linger. Skin-lightening creams are enthusiastically bought and sold on every single continent to those who don't have the "right" (read: white) skin tone. A painful, hours-long process exists for Black women to chemically straighten their hair so it looks more "professional" (read: white). Plastic surgeries are available to change the eyelids of East Asian women from monolids to "beautiful" (read: Western, white) eyelids. Even among white women there are standards to be upheld: large breasts, no cellulite, thin waists, straight teeth, clear skin, bleached assholes.

These standards didn't appear out of thin air. Someone, somewhere decided that they would hire a Black actress with Eurocentric features and light skin over a Black actress with wide hips and dark skin. And then another someone, somewhere did the same. And another, and another, and another. This has happened ad nauseam across every other possible category one can think of: race, gender, age, sexuality, body size, physical ability. This is how beauty becomes an imperial project: those who are considered "beautiful" according to these standards are also considered inherently more valuable than those who aren't. When a thin, pretty white girl like JonBenét Ramsey is found dead, it ignites fury and indignation that spans decades, still important enough to warrant cover stories in 2018 tabloids. When a gorgeous, award-nominated Indigenous actress just breaking it big in Hollywood named Misty Upham goes missing, the local police don't even look for her. Her family have to organize the search party themselves, eventually finding her body ten days after they file the missing person report. In a world where beauty equals worth, not being the right kind of beautiful has material consequences on the quality of your life — and your death.

That's what's so revolutionary about the rise of platforms like YouTube, Twitter and Instagram: the old gatekeepers are becoming obsolete. The only person that can decide who deserves to be seen and valued now is the person who is uploading content. This means that communities that were once considered below appealing to are visible in a way they never were before, which also means they can make their interests known in ways they never could before. And this increased visibility seems to be working.

Rihanna's beauty line Fenty Beauty launched in 2017 with a nearly unheard-of forty foundation shades, then proceeded to sell out of many of the darkest shades for months, sending an immediate message to the rest of the beauty industry: appeal to all skin tones — value all skin tones — or get left behind. *Black Panther,* which was written and directed by Ryan Coogler, a Black man, and featured an almost entirely Black cast, took in a box office total of $242.1 million on opening weekend, then sustained its success to become the third film in history to pass the $700-million mark in the U.S. This went against everything film executives claimed about the drawing power of Black directors and Black stars. It was no surprise to Black people, though, as they'd been anticipating the film for months, sharing photos and memes on Twitter and Instagram of themselves getting ready to see the film opening night. Conversely, the social media reaction to Hollywood films that have whitewashed characters of colour — casting Scarlett Johansson as a Japanese woman in *The Ghost in the Shell*, Emma Stone as a Hawaiian and Asian woman in *Aloha*, and Christian Bale as an Egyptian prince in *Exodus*, for example — coincided with poor domestic box-office performances. It would seem, then, that since social media is controlled by everyday people, allowing diverse viewpoints and representations to have a platform every second of every day, people no longer have to accept the discrimination of mainstream media and big industry.

It's important to remember that appealing to capitalism to fix the problems of racism, sexism, ageism, ableism, transphobia and homophobia is problematic in its own way. Capitalism always relies upon exploitation to create profit, and therefore it must always rely upon differing valuations of people's humanity. Still, every time I click on a #Native hashtag and see pride reflected back instead of shame, I know that we have a good start.

I recently came across a passage in Leo Tolstoy's essay "What Is Art?":

Art is not, as the metaphysicians say, the manifestation of some mysterious idea of beauty or God; it is not, as the aesthetical physiologists say, a game in which man lets off his excess of stored-up energy; it is not the expression of man's emotions by external signs; it is not the production of pleasing objects; and, above all, it is not pleasure; but it is a means of union among men, joining them together in the same feelings, and indispensable for the life and progress toward well-being of individuals and of humanity.

Selfies do that. Each person who posts a photo of themself online pushes back against imperial beauty standards and profit-driven gatekeepers, joining online communities that are built on our mutual understandings of how shame has impacted us. If posting selfies online means that we temporarily feel good about ourselves in a society that requires us to feel bad to make money; if it encourages us to refuse the idea that we need to change ourselves to fit impossible moulds, isn't that indispensable for our progress? Isn't it indispensable for our collective well-being?

"Through photographs, each family constructs a portrait-chronicle of itself —

a portable kit of images that bears witness to its connectedness."

Photographs are a family-building exercise. Sontag notes that children who are well photographed are assumed to be well loved. This is probably why my sister is still indignant that our parents took so few photos of her as a baby.

Recently, though, when going through a grey grocery bag of photographs my father's new wife salvaged from our old trailer, I saw a picture I'd never seen before — one that I didn't know existed, of a person I'd only learned existed the year before. The photo showed my mother holding a strange baby and smiling. Her smile wouldn't last. That strange baby was my half-sister, whom Mom had named Angelica. Soon after this picture was taken that baby would be pulled from her arms and carried away by adoption agents. My mother would never hold her again. She didn't want to be giving up Angelica. She was already a single mother of two when she had her, and she knew she couldn't care for Linnie, her first child, who had cerebral palsy and used a wheelchair, while also mothering both Teena and a newborn. She had to make a choice. She chose to give up her new baby.

My family had thick photo albums, full of relatives I'd known my whole life, sprinkled with others I'd never met. We had hundreds of photos of our family smiling and laughing, still nestled inside the flimsy envelopes the one-hour-photo gave us. These were the moments my parents chose to memorialize. This was the family my parents chose to memorialize. By keeping that photo of Angelica from us, my parents denied us memories. They denied us family. Our kit of images bore witness not only to our connectedness but also to our disconnectedness.

"As photographs give people an imaginary possession of a past that is unreal, they also help people to take possession of space in which they are insecure. Thus, photography develops in tandem with one of the most characteristic of modern activities: tourism."

Every tourist has taken pictures of the places they've travelled. I remember taking my camera to Niagara Falls for a trip with my husband and kid. All I wanted was to take pictures of them in this different space, candidly enjoying one another's company. I couldn't, because my kid was trained from infancy to pose for a camera and they've perfected posing to a fine art, but still. *I need to remember this,* I told myself, *and memory is unreliable, so I need photos.* It worked. I have those photos to bring myself back to specific points in time and space. There we are in one photo, our clothes protected by translucent, bright blue ponchos, our ponchos covered with water drops that shimmer in the sun as we stand on the *Maid of the Mist*'s lower deck. There's the Horseshoe Falls, where Lelawala, the Seneca woman considered the original Maid of the Mist, was saved by the god of thunder, then went on to save her village from a giant snake. There are all the other blue-clad families scrambling to get the perfect photo of the perfect falls. We're all trying to take home a piece of this natural beauty, even if it's just a picture.

I didn't take pictures of the homeless people panhandling. I didn't take pictures of the throngs of people, each street so full I was terrified my kid would get lost in the crowd, causing me to clutch their hand tighter. I didn't take pictures of the impoverished area surrounding the Greyhound bus terminal, which looked completely abandoned. I didn't take pictures of the cheap motel we were staying in. I was using photos to curate my ideal space, my ideal way of remembering this trip. Sontag refers to this use of photography as "a way of refusing [experience] — by limiting experience to a search for the photogenic, by converting experience into an image, a souvenir." In other words, photography and tourism work in tandem to make natural beauty a commodity, an experience that in a very real sense must be purchased to be enjoyed, then converted into a product, a photo.

So many people simply have no idea how to appreciate natural beauty without turning it into a picture. I felt this acutely the last time I was in Banff, Alberta. Banff National Park is the oldest national park in Canada — and it just so happens to be situated on Treaty 7 territory, the traditional homelands of the Stoney Nakoda, Blackfoot and Tsuut'ina Nations. I finally understood what the word "sublime" meant when I beheld its mountains, forests and lakes for the first time.

Realistically, the Rocky Mountains are stunning not only from the vantage point of Banff. They're stunning everywhere. But just like with Niagara Falls, capitalism has tied itself to the natural beauty of Banff

National Park, giving them reason to remain beautiful. Because this space can be turned into profit people will pay for entry to the park, hotel rooms in Banff, food and drink along the strip — the space is taken care of so that people will *want* to take pictures. After all, what else can they do with the space? It's not like most of the people who come put down tobacco at the water's edge, or give thanks to every element of creation within the space, the way we Haudenosaunee do with our Thanksgiving address.

None of the camera-clutching tourists seemed to wonder why this part of the Rocky Mountains is considered worth protecting while another part of the same mountain range, in B.C., as well as the Columbia Mountains and the Coast Mountains, which are all just as stunning, are currently being plundered to make room for the Kinder Morgan pipeline. None of them seem to find it unusual that they're allowed, even encouraged, to preserve the *memory* of the mountains with photographs, while those fighting to preserve *the actual mountains* for future generations are arrested and jailed. Now that the government of Canada has purchased the Kinder Morgan pipeline with $4.5 billion of taxpayers' money — without consulting Canadians, naturally —

the completion of this pipeline is a national project. The government can officially use whatever means necessary to ensure that these beautiful mountains are destroyed, the picturesque water around them is polluted, and the oil of a dying industry gets to wherever they want it to go.

When I think about what Indigenous nations are currently doing and will continue to do to stop this pipeline in Canada, it's hard not to reflect on the Standing Rock Sioux and their fight against the Dakota Access Pipeline. For over a year, from April 2016 to February 2017, this nation stood behind their youth, who were the first ones to voice opposition to the pipeline, which was to be built beneath two rivers and one lake. These youth started a movement, organized runs, engaged in direct action. Their fight for the water, their assertion that water is life, struck an emotional chord. Soon celebrities like actress Shailene Woodley and writer Naomi Klein were at the camp offering support — along with thousands of allies. There were solidarity marches, days of action, cities passed resolutions offering support for the Standing Rock Sioux. Two thousand veterans from the group "Veterans Stand for Standing Rock" offered themselves as human shields for protesters.

It didn't matter. There was money to be made, so private security teams used dogs and tear gas to attack protesters while police looked on and did nothing. Later, those same police turned water cannons on protesters in freezing temperatures, as well as tear gas, sound cannons, rubber bullets and concussion grenades. Protestor Sophia Wilansky nearly lost her arm after being hit by what she claims was a grenade. (Police have denied they used concussion grenades and claim Wilansky's injury was the result of an exploding propane canister.) I suspect variations of all of these tactics will be used on those trying to stop the Kinder Morgan Pipeline. Although we are told that police forces exist to protect the public, incidents like this show what the police really prioritize: protecting private corporations and profit, and therefore the nation-state. After all, if politicians didn't utilize state-funded forces to keep major corporate and private donors in the black, how else would they fundraise for their reelection campaigns? What's worse: so many of the people who actively work against Indigenous protesters — from the police officers to the politicians to the executives of oil companies — will go on vacations with their families to beautiful beaches, stare out at the pastel sunset after a refreshing swim, take photos of their kids silhouetted against the horizon to post to Facebook and Instagram, and not even for a moment reflect on their blatant hypocrisy.

In this age, the natural world is spared only if it can be photographed; if its beauty can be sold; if it doesn't get in the way of more pipelines and more profit.

"Like sexual voyeurism, [photographing] is a way of at least tacitly, often explicitly, encouraging whatever is going on to keep happening. To take a picture is to have an interest in things as they are, in the status quo remaining unchanged (at least for as long as it takes to get a 'good' picture) . . . including, when that is the interest, another person's pain or misfortune."

I took a photography course in high school. One of the assignments was a portrait series. All photos were supposed to be of the same person, but in different settings and perspectives. I chose my five-year-old brother, Dakota, for my subject. I followed him around with a camera I borrowed from school — down our long gravel driveway after checking the mail; near the creek by our house, where Dakota liked to go to think; into the dense woods on our family property. All of that was fine. None of it seemed exploitative.

But then Dakota got into a fight with one of our brothers and started to cry. I wanted to comfort him, but I also still needed to get a close-up photo of him, and the focused lighting of the lamp in my room would be perfect. I told Dakota to come to my room, let him lie on my pillow, adjusted the lamp and took picture after picture of his puffy, red face, adjusting the aperture between his sobs. Part of me wondered what he was feeling. He was crying, and his older sister, who was usually the first to console him after our mother, was taking pictures of him crying instead of soothing him. Did he feel he needed to keep crying for the sake of the pictures? Was he hurt that I seemed to care more about getting the perfect photo of him crying than him actually crying? I never asked, he never said. The same way I never asked myself why I could so easily turn off my concern for my own brother for the sake of "art."

The morality of and rationale for this type of photography — that is, photography featuring people in pain — becomes more fraught when these photos aren't meant to be art at all. In 2004, CBS published photos that members of the U.S. Army and CIA had taken of themselves committing human rights abuses against detainees in the Abu Ghraib prison in Iraq the year before. The photos appeared everywhere, featuring disgusting, unspeakable acts of torture and abuse against Middle Eastern men. I was disgusted, but I wasn't surprised. War crimes are common, and the dehumanization of Middle Eastern people started well before 9/11.

I do, however, question *why* the soldiers took pictures of the torture and abuse they were committing. Unlike with the Vietnam War, which Sontag references in her essay, the photographers of the torture at Abu Ghraib weren't war photographers. They were the soldiers themselves, often using personal cell phone cameras. What's more, these soldiers were not only choosing to abuse these men; they were also choosing to document their abuse of these men, and therefore furnish the very evidence that would eventually be used against them in disciplinary procedures. But to what ends? One can hardly imagine any person looking back fondly at these photos.

Sontag writes, "There is something predatory in the act of taking a picture. To photograph people is to violate them, by seeing them as they never see themselves, by having knowledge of them they can never have." Perhaps photography gave these American soldiers an additional layer of power over their Iraqi prisoners: the power to turn the prisoners' pain and humiliation into images without their consent, to forever "capture" them the way the soldiers saw them — as terrorists, as less than human.

Of course, that doesn't explain the presence of the American soldiers in the pictures, posing in photo after photo alongside the men they tortured. Which came first: the camera or the abuse? Did the camera's presence encourage the abuse to keep happening? Did the American soldiers in a sense "perform" their violence for the camera, attempting to stage the perfect pictures of torture? How would the abuse have changed if there was no camera? Or would it have changed at all?

It's somewhat frightening to think about the camera as intermediary. How much does the camera's physical presence between the soldiers (the photographers) and the prisoners (the photographed) create the type of distance necessary for the soldiers to still pretend they're good people? As if the very act of taking a photo — of viewing real life through a lens — somehow made whatever you were taking a picture of less real, less worthy of intervention or concern.

Maybe this is a version of what happened when I photographed my crying brother. Maybe there is no way to ethically photograph pain.

"Photographs can abet desire in the most direct, utilitarian way — as when someone collects photographs of anonymous examples of the desirable as an aid to masturbation. . . . Desire has no history — at least, it is experienced in each instance as all foreground, immediacy."

First things first: desire definitely has a history. Its history is intertwined with beauty standards that reinforce systemic oppressions — colonialism, sexism, racism, ableism, homophobia, transphobia — as well as being intertwined with rape culture, or, if you prefer, a culture of non-consent. The desire of cisgendered, heterosexual white men has not only been historically used to evaluate the worth of women, two-spirit people and non-binary folks; it has also been continually wielded as a weapon against us, targeting our respective bodies with sexual and physical violence, as well as murder and genocide. The idea that desire's "immediacy" somehow removes it from this specific, painful history is absurd. In fact, it is that very immediacy that often excuses violence against us, playing into the rhetoric that a violent man simply "couldn't help himself" or "got caught up in the moment."

It is with this history in mind that we should examine the rise in revenge porn and celebrity nude pic leaks, which I consider two sides of the same coin. Revenge porn is exactly what it sounds like: a man encourages a woman he's seeing to send him nude pictures of herself. She complies. When they break up, the man posts her nudes all over the internet without her consent.

The thing is, not all revenge porn is done after a breakup. When I was in university, I sometimes hung out with a group of guys my husband had befriended. They were all traditionally nerdy: liked video games, Star Wars, comic books, etc. Of the five or six of them, my husband was the only one in a relationship. I was always uncomfortable around them. It felt to me like they didn't see me as a person. They'd talk around me, never asking my opinion, some rarely acknowledging my presence at all. I tried telling this to my husband, but I didn't want to alienate him from his friends. I couldn't really put my finger on what was bothering me, anyway.

But then my husband found out that one of them had a new girlfriend and had shown the other guys her nudes. I immediately understood my discomfort. This man had been dating her for a short time and he already felt he had the right to share her body with his friends without her consent. Her body was a type of social capital for him, and sharing photos of it with his friends was a way of sharing — and flaunting — his wealth. These men were never outright rude to me when I was with them; their ignoring me wasn't any different than what I'd expected from most men. But if I'd taken a nude photo of myself and they saw it, would they see me as even more of an object and less of a human than they already did? Would their eyes glaze over as they looked, my image joining the ever-expanding library of naked women's images they'd catalogued in their minds? Would they tell themselves that looking at my photo was the same thing as looking at porn? At least porn stars know their photos will be looked at by strangers. At least they choose for their naked bodies to be photographed and for those photographs to be shared. Theoretically.

I thought about finding out who this man's girlfriend was and telling her what he'd done. I knew she had a right to know who she was dealing with, to protect herself. Instead, I distanced myself from this group of men, never saying a word to anyone about their revenge porn bonding session, making a promise to myself to not take nudes, not even for my husband — not because there is anything wrong with the photographs themselves but because you never really knew what a man would do with them, any man, even the man you trusted most in the world.

There really is no better term for it than "revenge porn" — even when the man who carries it out is still in a relationship with the woman he's exploiting, even when he doesn't have a reason to be enacting revenge. Every act of sharing pictures of a woman's body without her consent is an act of revenge. As with the (often male) hatred levelled at selfies, the hatred that leads someone to turn a private photo into revenge porn is a specifically misogynistic type of hatred. The woman is hated for daring to make a sexual photo of herself, despite the fact that often the man she's sending her picture to asked her to do it. The woman is hated for daring to control the way a man sees and experiences her body. For having sexual agency, for seeing herself as sexy, for having a sexuality independent of that man.

This is the same mentality that fuels the rabid demand for nude pics of celebrities. Every time a woman's private photos are leaked without her consent, straight men rejoice at a new trove of pictures to jack off to, collectively revelling in the violation necessary for these photos to be available — the violation that makes these photos so scintillating to them in the first place. They're sexier than the nude photos celebrities agree to pose for, or the love scenes they agree to appear in; they're more "dangerous." Why? Because the woman whose naked body you're looking at did not want you to see them. The immediacy with which hacked celebrity nude pics are posted to the internet and downloaded onto millions of hard drives, regardless of the immorality of it, says more about the connections between photography, desire, history and immediacy than anything else ever could.

After all, these men simply couldn't help themselves, could they?

"That most logical of nineteenth-century

aesthetes, Mallarmé, said that everything in the world exists in order to end in a book. Today everything exists to end in a photograph."

Photos — or the possibility of photos — are everywhere today in a way they most certainly weren't when Sontag wrote this line. Still, she seemed to anticipate the way that photographs would be used to validate people's lives, their very existences, in a way that had, until then, been unavailable.

While preparing to write this essay, I typed this into a memo on my cell phone: "Photo essay: Are our experiences made more real when they're witnessed?" I don't know if, in reading and rereading Sontag or writing and rewriting this essay, I've come any closer to answering this question. The easy answer is no, of course not. An event is real regardless of whether it's witnessed by anyone else. But the other, more complicated, answer is yes, others witnessing an event makes it more real. People seeing something happen both validates it and corroborates it. When an event is witnessed by someone else, you don't have to rely on your own (faulty, imperfect) memory to recall it. You can ask others about their memory of it, or — in the case of photographs — you can revisit an image in order to fill in the blanks. Ultimately, I think both of these answers are correct in different ways.

As I come to the end of this essay, though, I've realized that the more important questions about photography and its role in our world have very little to do with photography at all. The questions I keep coming to are questions about people, about us. Why do we need our lives to be witnessed? Why do we need to share our experiences, to have this connection to others? Why do we need to control others so badly and so completely that we will even try to control their image? Is it because we're trying to make ourselves more real? Is it because that power — as expansive or minuscule as it may be — fills a void?

Conversely, why don't we want to be witnessed? Why do we shrink from others' eyes? Why do we tell ourselves we don't deserve to be seen, on anyone's terms, even our own?

Maybe the reason everything exists to end in a photograph is because this world isn't equipped to offer something more meaningful: for everything to end in respect, acceptance and acknowledgement.

TWO TRUTHS AND A LIE

In my first undergraduate fiction workshop, our professor had us play Two Truths and a Lie, a game in which you share three statements about yourself and the rest of the group tries to determine which one is a lie. The idea behind the exercise was to help us figure out how to best utilize detail to make our fiction believable.

The game seems simple — until you realize most people don't have interesting facts about themselves stored away for when a whimsical get-to-know-you game erupts. Though our class was made up of aspiring writers, we seemed to forget our imaginations entirely within the constraints of the exercise. Instead, we relied on safe, sanitized facts that didn't reveal anything about us as people, but increased our chances of "winning" the game.

The trick was to take three boring facts about yourself and alter one just enough that it wasn't technically true, but sounded close enough that it was undetectable as a lie. For example, I could state that I was born in Amherst, New York, when I was actually born in Buffalo. This manipulation of truth is so slight that only an already-intimate knowledge of my life would give me away.

Lying by omission, slight bends of the truth, "little white lies" — we know that players will have a hard time telling these lies from the truth, because these are the same types of lies we tell every day while maintaining our images as inherently trust-worthy people. It's strange, but most people do seem to believe that other people are always telling them the truth — at least initially. Adrienne Rich writes about this phenomenon in her 1975 essay "Women and Honour: Some Notes on Lying":

> You tell me: "In 1950 I lived on the north side of Beacon Street in Somerville." You tell me: "She and I were lovers, but for months now we have only been good friends."

You tell me: "It is seventy degrees outside and the sun is shining."

[. . .]

I fling unconscious tendrils of belief, like slender green threads, across statements such as these, which have no tone or shadow of tentativeness. I build them into the mosaic of my world. I allow the universe to change in minute, significant ways, on the basis of things you have said to me, of my trust in you.

One wonders: why does Rich trust this person's account of anything? Why do we trust any person's account of anything? We can be lied to at any time, for any reason. Of course, to acknowledge this truth would lead to social decay. Without some semblance of trust, how could we build relationships, families, communities, cities, countries, governments, economies?

One place where lying is socially acceptable — and, furthermore, expected — is in fiction. As writers, we don't like to think of our works of fiction as lies — too much of a negative connotation. But in the most literal sense, fiction is a lie, even when it reveals essential truths. Indeed, Italian author Elena

Ferrante has written that the goal of literature is "to orchestrate lies that always tell, strictly, the truth." The trick to good fiction is telling convincing, consistent-enough lies that the artifice is either forgotten or ignored by the reader. It's expected that writers borrow from their own lives and experiences to create more realistic fiction — or more compelling lies, whichever you prefer.

In that same fiction workshop where I played Two Truths and a Lie, I drew on my own experiences of my postpartum body to write a short story about motherhood. There were details that I wouldn't have known to include if I hadn't given birth to a child myself. When you're pregnant, your abdominal muscles stretch to accommodate the baby; when there's no baby pushing against your muscles anymore, it takes them weeks to shrink back down and firm back up. After I gave birth, my tummy felt like Jell-O. It didn't matter if I laid down or sat up — when I pushed against my stomach my hand kept moving into my body. I felt like if I pushed far enough I'd eventually feel the soft of my internal organs. Though this bizarre bodily change wasn't something I'd heard other mothers mention, I knew it was something they would recognize, so when I decided to write about a character uncomfortable with being a mother, I wanted to use this detail.

My fiction class knew that I was a teen mother. I'd actually used that as one of my two truths, assuming people wouldn't believe it. They did, without hesitation. I tried not to think too hard about why. When I workshopped that story, my peers talked about how realistic the character was, how her pain and anger toward her husband and child were palpable. This reading should have been a compliment; after all, every writer wants to hear that their character feels real. But it didn't feel like a compliment.

I worried that the workshop had essentially turned into another game of Two Truths and a Lie. If my character and I had both been young mothers, what else did we share? Did I resent my child, too? Did I despise my husband for impregnating me, then taking on so little of the actual child-rearing? Did I feel like my life was a waste now that domesticity and motherhood consumed me? My character certainly did, and readers might think my portrayal of her was too good to simply be the product of imagination and talent. I was scared my peers thought she was a bad mother — and

I was one, too, for writing her.

This fear was perhaps paranoid, but not at all unfounded. In 2007, Scottish author, journalist and broadcaster Muriel Gray was a judge for the Orange Prize for Fiction, now called the Women's Prize for Fiction, which is awarded exclusively to women authors and continues to be one of the United Kingdom's most prestigious literary prizes. Reflecting on this experience for *The Guardian,* Gray remarks:

> [It's] hard to ignore the sheer volume of thinly disguised autobiographical writing from women on small-scale domestic themes such as motherhood, boyfriend troubles and tiny family dramas. These writers appear to have forgotten the fundamental imperative of fiction writing. It's called making stuff up.

Gray never explains how she knows that women writing "on small-scale domestic themes" are crafting "thinly disguised autobiography." She never interrogates why, exactly, she thinks these women aren't "making stuff up." She seems to assume that women writing about domesticity, motherhood, and family are essentially memoirists too cowardly to own their experiences. Let me remind you: Gray is a woman author who was tasked with judging one of the most prestigious literary awards for women in the world. If we can't even rely on her to believe that women can have an imagination, who can we rely on?

It's an interesting bind. If women choose to write on domestic themes and their prose isn't "literary" enough, their work is cast as "chick lit," which is a genre we are supposed to look down upon because it's explicitly, unapologetically written for women. If women choose to write on domestic themes and their prose is literary enough, though, their work is accused of being thinly-veiled autobiography, and therefore less skillful — as though there is no talent that goes into crafting fiction so convincing that readers are sure the writer had to experience everything in its pages herself.

I've taken to calling this "the autobiography assumption." Ferrante regularly faces the autobiography assumption with her internationally bestselling Neapolitan Novels. When Kristen Roupenian's 2017 short story "Cat Person" was published online by *The New Yorker* to viral acclaim, it was misread as memoir almost immediately, with many readers referring to it as an "article" on social media — despite the

272

word "fiction" printed in red at the top of the page. Apparently, it's easier to believe every woman writing is living out the lives of her various protagonists than to believe that women are capable of just as much imagination and talent as men.

In a Vulture article on autofiction, Christian Lorentzen describes the genre as inviting "readers to imagine they might be reading from something like a diary, where the transit from real life to the page has been more or less direct." In other words, auto-fiction isn't concerned with "making stuff up"; it's concerned with fashioning art out of the author's real life, blurring the line between what's real and what's not.

My first encounter with the genre was Sheila Heti's 2010 novel *How Should a Person Be?* I was fascinated by Heti's decision to name her protagonist after herself and her characters after her real-life friends, and to include transcriptions of dialogue and real emails — I thought it was genius, really. It reminded me of the ways women I knew talked about art and life and sex and men. I became mildly obsessed with the book, insisting that every woman I knew read it. There was something so refreshing about a woman intentionally, unapologetically crafting her real life into fiction — seemingly without caring at all whether it was "literary" or not, or whether anyone judged her by her fictional avatar. I was sure Heti wouldn't have cared if her classmates collapsed her narrator and herself in a fiction workshop. In fact, she did it for them.

While Heti's decision to blend fiction and real life wasn't necessarily a reaction to the autobiography assumption, her work still plays with and troubles this pervasive tendency in important and surprising ways. By forcing readers to make the connection between the author's real life and their fiction, Heti actively turns the reading experience into a 200-page game of Two Truths and a Lie. Which thoughts are Sheila Heti the author's, and which are Sheila Heti the character's? Is there a difference? After all, Sheila Heti the author is still coming up with Sheila Heti the character's thoughts, and therefore must be thinking them, at least obliquely. Using that logic, if Heti the character voices a judgment of Margaux the character, does that mean Heti the author is also judging Margaux the real person? When you fashion a character out of yourself, as Heti has, does that character really reflect you? Or does it reflect how you think of yourself? Or neither? Does anyone have enough self-awareness to accurately recreate themselves on the page? As an author, where do you draw the line between reality and fiction? What about as a reader?

Almost as interesting as Heti's book itself are the critical reactions to it. In an interview with *The Quietus,* Heti responds to the repeated use of the word "narcissistic" in reviews of her book: "In a lot of the criticism where that word is used, I'm not sure if the critics know what they're talking about: me, the book, the character, this culture, or what." Indeed, the inability to sift the truth from the fiction in Heti's book seemed to have an impact on not just how readers saw her work, but how readers saw her. One writer even called Heti a bitch — despite only having a fictional novel to base this judgment on (that writer later apologized).

How Should a Person Be? seems to make readers and critics alike very uncomfortable, because it does everything a novel by a woman isn't supposed to do: it actually acknowledges itself as a book from life, thus turning the autobiography assumption inside out; it centers women, depicting the rise and fall of the friendship of artists Sheila and Margaux, as well as Sheila's brutal sexual relationship with her lover

Israel; and it uses these relationships as the basis for philosophical musings on art, personality, sex and life.

While Muriel Gray could very well dismiss *HSAPB* as "thinly disguised autobiographical writing" about "drama" and "boyfriend troubles," I highly doubt she would refer to it as either "small-scale" or "domestic." *HSAPB* is simply too well-written and original to be dismissed in any of the usual ways books by women usually are. Thus, the continual, intellectually lazy reliance on condemning the book as "narcissistic," as though Heti's mining of her own life were any more narcissistic than the largely autobiographical — and canonical — novels of men like Ernest Hemingway or Jack Kerouac.

In an interview with *Tin House,* Heti said she would have preferred if the cover of the novel didn't include any references to it being "a book from life" or having used "real emails and transcriptions!" Of course, if her novel didn't have those things — if the characters had made-up names and the real emails and transcriptions Heti used were passed off as entirely fictional — it wouldn't have had the same voyeuristic appeal. The underlying promise of "reality" gave the entire novel additional weight that most other forms of fiction don't have: if any scene was real, if any conflict was real, then its inclusion could have real effects on Heti's real life. As a result, the book had built-in stakes beyond its own pages. Indeed, Heti hints in a *Guardian* interview, "I'd never write a book in this way again. I understand why people write fiction now. A lot of complications can arise. Fiction is a way for writers to preserve their friendships and their romances."

In 2018, Heti released her newest novel *Motherhood,* and this time there was no reference to it being "a book from life," no "Sheila, the character," no transcriptions of real emails. And yet Heti told *The Globe and Mail:*

"With *How Should a Person Be?* it was so clear to me that it wasn't me. And with this book, I feel a little more confused about it myself. I know that it's not me in the sense of how memoir would be me [. . .] it's kind of like what would have been in the background of my mind brought to the foreground, other things from the foreground pushed away. So it is a construction. But the thoughts are more or less mine."

Embarrassingly, when I read an advance

copy of the book, even I didn't realize it was fiction until I was halfway through. When I put the book down, the words "A Novel" stared up at me, defiant.

I started watching the reality TV show *Vanderpump Rules* because Rihanna tweeted about it — and because my friend assured me it was addictive and distracting in all the ways I needed at the time. *Vanderpump Rules* follows the lives, loves and fistfights of a group of servers and bartenders at the West Hollywood restaurant SUR, short for Sexy Unique Restaurant. SUR is owned and operated by the rich, fabulous Lisa Vanderpump, who acts as a sort of motherly figure to her stunning staff of would-be models, actors, and musicians. Since the restaurant is full of beautiful, insecure, jealous people, drama is all but inevitable.

There's cheating, drinking, screaming, dancing, vacations, more drinking, break ups, make ups, restaurant drama, failing and flailing entertainment careers, and even more drinking. Despite it being called reality TV, none of it is like any reality I know. My life is fairly uneventful. I spend most days in my pajamas, scrolling through Twitter and watching true crime documentaries. The staff of SUR, however, seem to be in a constant state of crisis and conflict. With each episode, I found myself wondering how these people could be so cruel to one another, even as I savoured the opportunity to peek in on that cruelty.

I couldn't understand why I was so drawn the show. My friend suggested it was cathartic to see people unabashedly acting out in ways we knew we shouldn't. And it was. But I also felt there was something more to it, as though the very spite with which the cast treats one another has its own magnetism.

Everything about *Vanderpump Rules* is pure spectacle — from the sexy staff to the restaurant to the luxury suites Vanderpump secures for cast vacations. Whenever an episode ended and I saw a preview of the next episode, my decision to continue binging depended on the degree of spectacle advertised. If one of the Toms was throwing a drink on one of their girlfriends, I was in. If everyone looked like they were getting along well enough, I'd take a break. The more these people hurt one another, the more I wanted to watch them hurt one another.

The show relies on that reaction. Like many reality TV shows, *Vanderpump Rules* uses spectacle and cruelty to attract and maintain its viewers. According to Varun Duggirala, who has produced Indian reality

TV shows *Get Gorgeous* and *Kidnap,* "All people working on reality TV have a sadistic side to them [. . .] people crying tends to give you a sense of satisfaction." While on paper this admission sounds disgusting, it makes sense. I would definitely watch another episode of *Vanderpump Rules* if I saw someone crying in a preview. I wonder, though: how do the contestants feel knowing that their pain is my pleasure? That the more stress they're under, the more people will watch their show? How does it feel knowing that their livelihood now depends on how well they can emote for the cameras?

SUR bartender and *Vanderpump Rules* cast member Jax Taylor has said in interviews,

I pride myself on [the fact that] we have a real show and I'm not going to sit there and sugarcoat things [. . .] Just because there are cameras I'm not going to be like, 'Oh, I'm going to do this and act like this.'

Jax has been arrested for shoplifting, cheated on every one of his girlfriends, had sex with his best friend's girlfriend, gotten into fights with total strangers, and has been referred to as a "sociopath" numerous times. His cruelty pushes each person on the show to the point where they eventually stop caring about the cameras altogether, offering a more "real" performance of their pain. And his pay reflects that. According to reports, after Vanderpump herself, Jax has the highest salary of all cast members at a whopping $25,000 per episode. He's also been rewarded with a spin-off show with his current fiancé called *Vanderpump Rules: Jax and Brittany Take Kentucky.* He is reportedly worth $500,000 — all for treating his friends and lovers like shit on television.

Knowing that those who are especially prone to blow ups and conflicts are featured more heavily on the show, and therefore paid a salary that reflects their impact on ratings, one has to question who these people are when the cameras are turned off. Is Jax playing an asshole for professional gain, or is the show emboldening him to indulge in his worst tendencies? Or do the two feed one another until you can't tell where the truth ends and the lie begins?

As I watched *Vanderpump Rules,* I found myself thinking about Heti's book again, which she crafted with another reality TV show, *The Hills,* in mind. Just as the characters in *How Should a Person Be?* are based on real people, the casts of *The Hills* and *Vanderpump Rules* are also based on real people. It's tempting to buy into the fantasy and believe that the people we see onscreen are the real people, but once the TV crew appears, the cameras turn on, the producers start whispering in people's ears and the editors begin manipulating footage, how real can anyone be?

At the same time, if your partner reveals to you that they're cheating on you while your lives are being filmed, how can you possibly keep that pain hidden from the cameras? How can you reign in your emotions and keep control of your image? We can only suppress pain and anger for so long; once that threshold is crossed, what others think of you doesn't matter. Cameras don't matter. All that matters is expressing your rage and agony.

If we were to break down a show like *Vanderpump Rules* into a game like Two Truths and a Lie, would the cast be able to distinguish truths from lies?

As a society, we're so used to heavily edited and manufactured reality that our ability to discern between truth and fiction is suffering. A Pew Research Center study found that only 17 percent of those over 65 could tell the difference between fact and opinion. It's not just the older generations, either: a 2016 Stanford study of middle school, high school and university students found that, "When it comes to evaluating information that flows through social media channels, they are easily duped."

I don't think it's a coincidence that these developments have come nearly 20 years after *Survivor* ushered in what *The Washington Post* has called "the era of reality TV." For almost two decades, reality TV has presented heavily manipulated narratives — all while telling us that what we're watching is "real." *Survivor* allegedly uses body doubles to stand in for contestants during physical challenges. *Storage Wars* producers purchase storage units in advance, then plant valuable items inside for the cast to win. Spencer Pratt and Heidi Montag from *The Hills* revealed that they had to shoot a scene where Montag thought she was pregnant 15 times before producers were satisfied with Pratt's faux anger. The mansion the Kardashians pass off as their home on *Keeping Up With The Kardashians* is actually an empty house turned into a set.

It's not hard to see a correlation between the falseness of reality TV and the recent rise of fake news. We've all witnessed the era of reality TV, watched as the line between reality and fiction has blurred before our eyes, leaving us amused, but ultimately unconcerned. Considering how easy it has been for people and foreign governments to manipulate social media sites like Facebook, Twitter, Reddit and 4chan to influence Western politics and spread false conspiracy theories, perhaps we should have been less amused and more concerned.

In the lead-up to the 2016 Republican primaries, media-planning and analytics firm AMG did an online poll of Republican voters after their candidates debated on CNN. In addition to asking who they thought won the debate, AMG also asked whether the person being polled watched *The Apprentice* or *The Celebrity Apprentice,* the reality TV shows that subsequently-elected US President Donald Trump had hosted for 11 years. His favourable rating among viewers of *The Apprentice* was a staggering 62 percent, whereas those who didn't watch the show rated him at only 37 percent. It didn't matter that he had no political experience, or that he has filed for bankruptcy six times, or that he has never released his tax returns. They saw Trump "playing an uber businessman and master manager for an hour a week on reality TV," as CNN political commentator David Axelrod put it, and that's precisely who Trump was to them.

Of course, that's not to say that Trump's business experience hasn't been valuable in his rise to the presidency. In an interview with PBS, journalist Gwenda Blair, who authored *The Trumps: Three Generations of Builders and a President,* explains:

> Salesmen are performers. They target their market. What does the market want to hear? [. . . Trump] would tell the market, in his first project, which was the Grand Hyatt, a hotel, [that] it was the biggest ballroom in New York. It wasn't but people liked the idea.

This "exaggerated hyperbole," which Blair claims is Trump's brand, would be classified by most people as lies. Since his inauguration, he has lied so often on Twitter and in the news that *The Washington Post* has started to keep track; as of the writing of this essay, Trump has made 6,420 "false or misleading claims" in 649 days, or approximately nine lies per day. In any other era, Trump's evident dishonesty, coupled with the absurd number of scandals he has been involved with, would have had him impeached far sooner, maybe even with tangible results on the presidency. But we are in the era of reality TV. The rules are different now, and Trump is not only aware of that, he's been depending on it.

The spectacle of reality TV — the same cruelty and drama and backstabbing that I love so much about *Vanderpump Rules* — has fundamentally shifted the way that we interpret and respond to the world around us. We've become accustomed to escalating public drama and escalating cruelty in ways we never have been before. We expect it, even crave it. And, if recent history has shown us anything, eventually, we come to accept it, even when we shouldn't. In true reality TV fashion, Trump has utilized his cruelty to get what he has always wanted most: attention. Whenever he has made offensive statements on Twitter or on TV, he hasn't been deplatformed or challenged. He hasn't been ignored. He's been rewarded with even more media attention. Just like Jax from *Vanderpump Rules,* the worse Trump has treated people, the more he has gained. The problem, of course, is that Trump hasn't just gained a spinoff show or a higher salary for next season; he has gained the most powerful position in the world.

We're living in a time where truth is less valuable than attention. Mainstream media outlets offering outrageous, offensive, click-bait editorials to outrageous, offensive, click-baity human beings; allowing pundits to argue marginalized peoples' humanity; offering a false equivalence between opinions that have no basis in truth and those that do; continuously hiding behind the rationale that we must hear "all sides" of an issue — it's the new normal, world-wide. And because it sells advertisements it won't change. Under capitalism advertisers pay for ad space on the websites, newspapers, and broadcast stations with the largest audience, not the most moral integrity. FOX News is currently considered the "King of Cable," celebrating 67 consecutive quarters as the highest-rated cable network in the U.S. as of October 2018. It was also deemed the least accurate news source on cable by PolitiFact in 2015, and has paid out thousands of dollars in lawsuits for falsely reporting Conservative conspiracy theories as facts. Truth doesn't garner attention the same way lies do, and as such news stations today must choose between reporting responsibly and staying in business.

Knowing this, can we be surprised when they invite white supremacists to give speeches at the New York Times Food Festival, or the Munk Debates, or on CNN and CBC? Can we be surprised that white nationalist and Toronto mayoral candidate Faith Goldy came in third in one of the most diverse cities in the world? After all, when people like this thrive on attention, even Tweets from opponents pointing out their racism, sexism, transphobia or xeno- phobia will inevitably feed them. Like any savvy reality TV star, the Gavin McInneses, Donald Trumps, and Faith Goldys of the world know that the worse they treat people, the more drama they create, the higher their profiles and the bigger their salaries. All we ever give them is our eyes and ears — but unfortunately, that's enough.

I've spent most of 2018 reading essays and creative nonfiction by marginalized people who see the way the tide has been turning against us. I can see it too. And it is frighten- ing. Every time negative news comes out about Trump, right-wing pundits spin it into a Liberal conspiracy instead of engaging with it as an inconvenient, unavoidable truth. Every time a media personality says something that demonizes and dehuman- izes an entire group of people, critics and supporters alike watch as the implications of that hatred are dismissed using the same "free speech" defense white nationalists have weaponized so well. I see how the era of reality TV had given rise to the era of post-truth politics and provocative hate mongers, creating a marketplace out of attention and outrage.

I'd always thought the secret to winning Two Truths and a Lie was in keeping your lies small. But really, it has nothing to do with the magnitude of the lies you tell — it's about what you can convince other people to believe.

Here are three statements that can be divided into two truths and a lie:

1. News organizations monetize hatred and outrage for ratings and ad revenue.
2. There are groups of people who deserve pain, suffering, even death, simply for existing.
3. For marginalized people, free speech has rarely, if ever, existed.

My two truths and your two truths may be different. My lie and your lie might be different. Which statements will you allow yourself to believe?

EXTRACTION MENTALITIES

This is a participatory essay. Think of it as a survey of sorts, or perhaps a conversation I'm trusting you to finish. The essay is done only when you consider it finished. I tried to write it without your help but, quite simply, I don't have all the answers — even if I sometimes might imply that I do.

The way it will work is this: every so often I will stop this essay to ask you questions. I'll leave space for you to answer. Do with that space whatever you will. Even blank spaces speak volumes.

The most terrifying villains have always been two-dimensional. They have no complex motivations, no sympathetic backstories detailing their own personal traumas. Their inner lives are unknown, unknowable. All we know is they're hell-bent on destruction.

Perhaps the best example of this type of

villain is Michael Myers, the serial killer in John Carpenter's 1978 classic, *Halloween.* At the age of six, Myers murders his older sister, Judith. At the age of twenty-one, he escapes a mental hospital so he can murder the first pretty, young babysitter he sees, Laurie Strode, along with every person who stands in his way. For most of the film we don't see his face; his eyes are black pits set deep within a white, featureless mask. He's cold, cruel, monstrous. Even demonic. When his child psychiatrist, Dr. Sam Loomis, calls Myers "pure evil," we believe him. After all, we've seen no evidence to the contrary. And it would seem the filmmakers agree: in the closing credits, Myers's character isn't even given a human name. He's listed only as "The Shape."

Abusers often get talked about the same way Myers does: as though they, too, are pure evil; not humans, but human shapes. Articles on abusers will detail their manipulation tactics, or their intense, singular selfishness. You might read click-bait listicles on narcissism and sociopathy — two traits common among abusers — with ominous warnings typed out at the top of the page. "Don't Let Yourself Get Manipulated!" they caution. "10 Red Flags That Could Save You from Getting Hurt." As if abuse were so easy to avoid. As if all you had to do was take one look at a person, then politely decline, the way one does when a waiter accidentally brings over the wrong dish. "I'm so sorry, but that's not what I ordered." Send it back to the kitchen. Smile at your tablemates. Move on with your life.

I know this isn't true. I've known abusers my whole life. Yet even I find myself tempted by the idea of this two-dimensional villain. Abusers aren't friends or family members or people you love; they're shadowy figures peeking around bushes, stalking their prey, the way Myers stalked Laurie on her way home from school. They're not people who can support or nurture or love; they only traumatize and destroy and ruin, leaving bloodied bodies and broken psyches in their wake. Good and evil. Right and wrong. These dichotomies are seductive because they're so simple. But that's also why these sorts of dichotomies will never create the change we need. They're too damn simple.

According to the National Intimate Partner and Sexual Violence Survey, approximately one in three women and one in three men in the United States have experienced contact sexual violence, physical violence, and/or stalking by an intimate partner in their lifetime. Knowing this, can you think of members of your family or any of your friends who have experienced abuse?_____

Can you think of members of your family or any of your friends that have been accused of being abusive?_____

If yes, how did you react when you found out? Are you still close with the accused abuser today?_____

If no, how do you reconcile the statistics above with what you think you know about those close to you?_____

Have you ever wondered why women in abusive relationships stay with their abusers?

If your answer to the last question is "yes," please revisit the third and fourth questions.

My father enrolled me in a basketball league when I was in seventh grade. A Catholic one, naturally. Being involved with anything Catholic helped ease my mother's fears that my siblings and I were being morally corrupted by modern society.

Drives to basketball practice weren't long, but they were long enough to get in some good conversation with my dad. He always seemed more approachable then. It was as if the act of driving consumed all the energy he normally required to maintain the masculine, intimidating aura he wore so well. When he was behind the wheel, he was vulnerable. When he was behind the wheel, I could be vulnerable, too.

This particular night I was having problems with my best friend and next-door neighbour, Sam. Desirability politics had shut her out of the hormone-fuelled coupling most teens think determines their worth. Beauty standards had declared Sam both fat and unattractive, so she was left to watch as brainwashed boys settled for me, her thinner, kind-of-cute-but-definitely-not-sexy friend. I can only imagine how much this got to her. A boy she had a crush on and started chatting up at a roller rink completely diverted the conversation by telling her he was interested in me. That was awkward enough, but then she pressured me to date him despite my never speaking a word to him. I was confused, but agreed, the way I agreed any time Sam asked me to do anything. Suffice it to say, our whirlwind romance didn't last.

Throughout our friendship, Sam had a habit of implying I was ugly, or emphasizing how poor I was, or making digs at my weight that left me feeling worthless. This upset me, but I didn't want to talk about it with my mom. She wasn't a big fan of Sam and seemed poised to pounce on any excuse for me to cut ties with her. That left my dad and our drive to basketball practice, his eyes focused on the white lines of the street.

"I just don't understand why she's like this," I said. "I don't say anything like that to her."

"She has an inferiority complex," my dad replied, his voice so confident I immediately knew it must be true.

"What's that?"

"You're beautiful, talented and smart. She worries she's not any of those things, so she tries to make herself feel better by tearing you down. I've known a lot of people like that."

At the time this seemed the most logical thing I'd ever heard. Of course she had an inferiority complex. Of course. It made so much sense. The world had finally slid into focus.

I looked at my father, wondering where he'd learned this. His quiet demeanour revealed nothing, but it didn't have to. The knowledge was enough. I turned and watched the blackened streets fly by my window, a calm settling my anxious gut. I held on to my father's words every time Sam cut me down after that night, which happened with disappointing regularity until my family moved two years later. I held on to his words throughout high school and university, through workplace issues and relationship blunders. I still hold on to his words now. Sometimes you're not the problem. Sometimes it's another person's insecurity that's the problem, and that person decides that rather than fix the problem, they'd rather take everything out on you.

After reading the anecdote above — a story of my father alternately praising and counselling me; a story I cherish and will always remember fondly — would you assume my father was the villain I was writing this essay about? Why or why not?_____

Memories are strange. After a certain point you don't remember the actual event you experienced anymore. You remember your memory of that event. Certain details fall away while others loom large. Dialogue distorts. Cause-and-effect chains tangle and twist.

To further complicate matters, people have a tendency to filter out memories to reinforce certain ideas. In those cases, what stands out and what gets buried depends on the story you're crafting with your memories. For example, if I wanted to tell you about how much my father supported my dream to become a writer, all my memories of his abuse and neglect would fall away. I'd bring up one of the countless times he's sent me links to contests or writing opportunities, things he researched specifically for me. I'd go into detail about the way he used to talk me up to the editor of our local rez paper, using his friendship with her to try to help me get my foot in the door. I'd tell you about the time he was sitting in a doctor's office reading one of my essays from a literary journal I sent him and the man next to him asked about it. I'd tell you how, when the man said he was interested in writing an autobiography but didn't know where to start, my father put my essay in his hands, made him read it, then told him I could help him write his story — for a considerable fee. My father has always expressed his love by offering unsolicited, unconventional opportunities to me, the type that can only be dreamed up and brokered by the best, most innovative salesmen. My father is nothing if not a salesman. His unshakable faith nourished me, made me believe in myself and my talent when life gave me so many reasons not to. That's love.

But loving someone also means letting your guard down around them. It means revealing the harshest, angriest, most wounded parts of yourself. Sometimes that's ugly. Sometimes it leaves bruises. Sometimes it draws blood. Not just metaphorically. If I wanted to tell you a story about that, I'd tell you that one of my earliest memories is my father holding me against the wall by my throat, my feet dangling above the cold cement of our basement floor. I'd tell you how my older sister screamed at him to let me go and how my father, surprisingly, listened, dropped me, turned, then backhanded her, sending her to the ground. The memory ends there. There's no resolution, no *deus ex machina* that swoops in to save us. We were hurt. We were alone.

The strange thing is my father never abused people he didn't like. He never snapped at the racist manager who promoted the less talented white salesmen around him. He never choked my mother's brother for stealing his beloved, expensive stereo system. He saved that for us — for the ones he said he loved. Did he still love

298

us when he hurt us? Or did he hurt us because he loved us? Maybe for him love was a fire that could both warm and burn, encouraging him to become both his best self and his worst self.

Have you ever hurt people you love? If so, please explain why._____

When I want to remember the good things about my father, I must forget the bad things. When I want to remember the bad things about him, I must forget the good. There's no space for me to hold both of these realities at the same time, no grey logic in this black-and-white world. There are either heroes or villains. Victims or abusers.

These dichotomies must remain intact.

And yet.

Toronto-based Anishinaabe and Métis writer Gwen Benaway writes, "The truth about survivors is that we come from other survivors, are woven into a history of violence and rupture as long as we have stories for." My father is a survivor. He survived his father. He's surviving colonialism. He's also currently surviving a particularly brutal battle with prostate cancer, for which he has refused chemotherapy in favour of things like hemp oil and a more balanced diet. I know he's in pain because I've looked it up. Prostate cancer causes dull, deep pain in the lower back or pelvis. Sometimes the pain reaches down into your thighs or up into your ribs. There's weight loss. Appetite loss. Nausea. Vomiting. Swelling in your feet. Dad never lets on that he's hurting. When I ask him about his health, he mumbles a dismissive line or two, waving concern away with the flustered annoyance of an over-mothered child. He knows how to survive. He's always known how to survive. Why should I bother him with my fear or doubt now?

I wonder whether he's treated his own trauma the same way. We've never talked about how his father abused him, for instance. I only know about it because my mother would make vague comments explaining away Dad's outbursts or rationalizing his anger. In these conversations, abuse created a butterfly effect; a ripple in childhood could create a hurricane in adulthood. If Dad's experiences of abuse made him hurt us and our family, how were our experiences of abuse going to make us hurt our own families? I watched Dad for hints that he was still hurting from his childhood.

Watched him in the car while he was driving. Watched him while he set up our inflatable pool in the backyard. I never saw what I expected to see. I only saw him.

Once, while Dad was cutting down a tree for firewood, the chainsaw stopped working. A small piece of wood was trapped in the chain. Dad pulled the wood out with his fingers. As soon as he did, the chainsaw started up again, ripping into his flesh and nearly cutting off the tip of his index finger. He'd forgotten to turn the chainsaw off. When he came into the house, damp, dark red fabric wrapped around his hand, my mother screamed. Dad insisted he was fine, became annoyed when Mom insisted on driving him to the hospital. He was obviously hurt, but his face was calm. His face showed no fear, no pain. It was the face he always wore.

It wasn't until I was older that I considered what this could mean. Maybe I couldn't map the pain on his face because he was always in pain.

Last year, a friend asked me about my father. I told her a condensed history of the way he treated my loving, brilliant mother. I explained how my father's physical, mental, emotional, spiritual, financial and verbal

301

abuse of her influenced the way I viewed her, the way I viewed myself, and the way I viewed mental illness. As the words came out of my mouth I could see my friend trying to mask her disgust. Still my voice was steady, nonchalant even. I detailed some of my most painful memories as though they hadn't affected me at all, even when I was explaining the precise ways they had. Apparently I had taken on his impartiality to pain, as well.

When I was finished, my friend asked me why I still spoke to him. I didn't know what to say. Why did I still speak to my father? It seemed insufficient to merely say that I loved him, though of course that was true. I did love him. I do.

But is my love for him, my continued relationship with him, enabling him to continue the same abusive behaviours that hurt our family? Should I cut him off for the things he's done — things he's shown no remorse for? Would that teach him to be better?_____

How long did it take you to come up with an answer to those questions? Or did you come up with answers at all?_____

I recently stumbled across a blog post analyzing the ways estranged parents interact with one another on message boards. Apparently, none of them have any idea why their children have decided to cut off all contact with them. Or at least that's what they initially claim. Slowly, though, the story trickles out, revealing that they do, in fact, know why their children don't want them in their lives anymore.

The problem is that these message boards are run by other estranged parents. They're supposed to be "supportive," but their idea of "support" is much different from my idea of support. I would have assumed a supportive message board for estranged parents would be a space where they could help one another identify and change their own abusive behaviours so they could eventually repair their relationships with their children.

Instead, the users of this message board spent a lot of time reading one another's stories and reinforcing the idea that none of them have ever done anything wrong. They rarely questioned another estranged parent's account of events. They didn't acknowledge contradictions in the statements they made to one another, or point out the ways they held their children to standards they refused to let their children or anyone else hold them to. If you were to read the comments they made to one another, you'd get the impression that all of their estranged children and grandchildren were selfish, ungrateful, illogical, even abusive.

I felt sick reading the posts, wondering if those were the sort of things my father would say about me if I decided to cut him off. He'd hold up all the good he's done for me, hide away the bad, and I would suddenly become another selfish, ungrateful, illogical, even abusive child in what appeared to be a sea of such children.

The blog showed that, for these estranged parents, context didn't matter. Their children's feelings and boundaries didn't matter. The only thing that mattered was what they felt at any given moment. It was as if these people all lived in an alternate reality where nothing they did had any repercussions but everything everyone else did had outsized ones. If you told them that they made you feel bad, it wasn't their fault — it was your fault for misunderstanding what they had meant. And at the same time, telling them they were making you feel bad made *them* feel bad, and there was no excuse for your treating them so terribly. In other words, being held accountable for abuse by the people they've abused was, in fact, abusive.

Have you ever encountered a person who thought being held accountable was abusive?_____

Have you ever been the person who thought being held accountable was abusive?_____

Is the line between abuser and victim becoming more blurry to you the more we discuss this? Why or why not?_____

Gaslighting is an abuse tactic by which a person manipulates another person into questioning their own sanity. Since I learned the term, I've realized the extent to which my father used this tactic on my family. He eventually took all of us to an abuse shelter on the rez because he claimed our mother was abusing him. The shelter believed it and let him in.

Part of me knew this was wrong, but the other part believed my father. He was so good at making sure we saw what he wanted us to see. The only time my mother seemed angry at my father's abuse was when she was manic. She'd point at him while spitting her testimony, thrust her index finger into his chest or shove him backwards with a hand. As soon as she did any of these things, Dad would yell, "Owwwww! Stop it! You're hurting me!" and we'd rush in, yelling at Mom to leave him alone. Sometimes I'd push myself between them, sure that she wouldn't hurt me on her way to him. It didn't occur to me at the time, but he only ever seemed to feel pain at these exact moments. In this way, my dad used my mother's mental illness to make her seem like the abusive parent. He even convinced me to write a statement about a fight they got into when she was manic, which he used to get full custody of us while Mom was in the mental hospital. I was thirteen. I had no idea what that meant. I had no idea what it meant until it was too late.

I never saw my father hit my mother. I came close once when we were going to church. Mom was so depressed she was scared to leave the house. Dad, furious, rushed back in to get her. I didn't see what happened before he took off and left us at home, but I did see her head bleeding at the hairline. I saw her glazed eyes. I heard her whimpering.

I don't know if my father remembers this. I don't know if he remembers any of it. Maybe he doesn't. Maybe he only remembers the emotions he was feeling when my mother wouldn't leave the house, or the emotions he's feeling now that I'm bringing this memory up. Maybe he can't do anything but gaslight me.

Does this feel like an explanation, or an excuse? Is there a difference?_____

In writing about the ways my father gaslit me, and offering only select memories and one perspective, does it feel like I'm gaslighting you? Manipulating you?_____

If we can't even get abusers to acknowledge the ways they're abusing others, how can we ever end abuse?

This is not a question I expect you to answer. It's just a question I've been asking myself. Particularly since so many discussions around how to deal with abuse tend to focus on the individual. If you're a victim of abuse, you simply need to get away from your abuser and you'll be fine. You simply need to cut them off and you'll be fine. And perhaps you will be.

But as a society, does telling abuse victims to get away from their abusers really address the causes of abuse? Does it stop the abuser from abusing others? Does it feel like it's solving the problem, or ignoring it?_

The books I've read about abuse usually present domestic violence as an individual problem instead of a societal problem. The authors will explain that abusers usually started off as victims, but when they say that, they tend to mean the abuser was once a victim within an abusive family. That's where the analysis ends. They don't take that logic a few steps further to situate domestic violence within the larger historical context of state violence, looking at the ways that the state specifically victimizes and abuses homeless people, racialized people, LGBTQ2S+ people, women, children and gender non-conforming people, disabled people, mentally ill people, poor people, and those who embody all possible configurations of those identities, in order to further its own agenda. The authors rarely investigate or interrogate the ways that Western cultural values actually encourage these abusive behaviours, even if Western laws (technically) discourage them.

Let me use my own experiences, my family and my nation's history as an example. As I've mentioned, my family experienced violence and abuse, but that violence and abuse didn't start in my family, or even in my parents' families, or their parents' families. You need to follow the thread back.

So let's go back. Way back. On Turtle Island, and specifically within Haudenosaunee communities, domestic violence was not an issue before contact. Our clan families lived in the same longhouse together, so you couldn't hide the way you were treating your wife and children. Everyone knew. In addition, after marriage, men would move into their wife's family longhouse, so her family members were continually monitoring the relationship and looking out for the wife and children. If you were found to be abusive, your belongings would be left outside of the longhouse and you would have to return to your clan's longhouse. For the worst offenders of violence in the community, one of the harshest punishments was expulsion from the community. That was almost always a last resort.

At the same time in Britain, then eventually in Canada and the U.S., families lived in private homes. Every member of the family was considered the personal property of the man of the house. Things that happened behind closed doors stayed there. It would be considered rude to ask a man how he treated his family, since that was his private business. After 1850, domestic violence slowly began to be outlawed, with wife beating made illegal in every U.S. state by 1920. Intimate partner violence against men didn't start getting major attention until the 1980s — a fact that underlines how we unfortunately continue to see men as unabuseable. Still, even with these laws on the books, arrests for domestic violence remain rare. Today in Canada, only two-thirds of those who are charged with domestic violence are convicted — and that doesn't even take into account the 47 percent of sexual assaults and 40 percent of incidents where women are beaten, choked, or assaulted with a weapon that are never reported to police.

In America, that rate is quite different thanks to the Violence Against Women Act (VAWA), which was signed into law in 1994 by then-President Bill Clinton — a man who was himself accused of sexual harassment and sexual assault four years after signing this bill (though Clinton denies these claims). The Violence Against Women Act set aside $1.6 billion for investigating and prosecuting domestic violence cases, imposed automatic and mandatory restitution to victims from those convicted, and allowed related civil suits to move forward even if prosecutors didn't take those cases to court. As a result, while most domestic violence cases in the U.S. get dropped, those that do make it to trial are more likely to result in a conviction, and domestic violence rates after its implementation have gone down a staggering 72 percent between 1994 and 2011.

This bill needs to be renewed regularly, and unfortunately every time that additions are proposed to protect more people under this act, Republican politicians have stalled it. In 2012, this happened when it was suggested the act's provisions be extended to protect same-sex couples and allow battered undocumented immigrants access to temporary visas. In 2019, this was because new provisions were created to protect trans people under VAWA, as well as to ban those convicted of domestic violence from purchasing firearms. As of this writing, the renewal of VAWA has still not passed the U.S. Senate.

Because both Canada and the U.S. are carceral states, those who are caught committing domestic violence are put through the court system. If found guilty, expulsion from the community in the form of incarceration is often the first resort, not the last, and can last a maximum of five years. In jail, abusers are not rehabilitated and taught better ways to deal with their pain, how to be better partners, or how to deal with the abuse they've experienced in their lives. Instead, they're treated as subhuman and often forced to perform manual labour for the state or select corporations, particularly in private prisons, for little to no money. In other eras, the word for this economic and moral arrangement was "slavery," but nowadays this is labelled "justice." We believe this treatment is what these people deserve.

Quite the difference.

My mother has called the cops on my dad for abuse. My father has called the cops on my mom for abuse. They've both been arrested for domestic abuse at various times. While no charges were laid and no trials had to be endured, the criminal justice system that was supposedly in place to protect us didn't help my parents, or our family. Instead it cast a shadow over our lives, making me afraid of police, lawyers, judges.

Has dealing with the criminal justice system helped anyone you know? If so, how?_____

Do you think the threat of imprisonment

keeps people from being honest about ways they've abused others?_____

Would you admit to abusing someone if admitting it meant you'd be imprisoned?___

Let's move out a bit. Let's think about how nation-states such as Canada and the U.S. are formed. For a nation-state to exist, for capitalistic wealth to exist, you need land. The settlers who landed here knew this. When they spoke of this land's beauty in their journals and letters, they weren't respecting the land as a beautiful, autonomous entity, or admiring the interconnected relationships between it and the animals, plants, waters and people it nourished. They certainly weren't interested in taking up their responsibilities to this land, ensuring it remained pristine for their descendants seven generations into the future.

They were concerned with capitalistic ownership. They wanted to suck up everything they could possibly take, regardless of future consequences, and turn it into material wealth — ostensibly for their countries, but realistically for a select few who would benefit much, much more than the average citizen. This is what I'll call extraction mentality. Leanne Betasamosake Simpson writes that "extraction is a cornerstone of capitalism, colonialism, and settler colonialism. It's stealing. It's taking something, whether it's a process, an object, a gift, or a person, out of the relationships that give it meaning, and placing it in a non-relational context for the purposes of accumulation."

Under capitalism, colonialism and settler colonialism, everything Indigenous is subject to extraction. Words from our languages are extracted and turned into the names of cities, states, provinces or, in the case of Canada, an entire country. Resources from our traditional territories are extracted and turned into profit for non-Indigenous companies and strategic political donations. Our own children are extracted so that non-Indigenous families can have the families they've always wanted, so our families will fall to ruin and our grief will distract us from resisting colonialism.

Then, after all of this extraction, the nation-state has the audacity to tell us we should be glad, that the theft was for our own good. Or, more recently, politicians will admit that awful things were done, but that they happened in the past and should be forgiven, despite modern-day equivalents still taking place all around us.

314

■ ■ ■

When you Google the word "abuse," you get "to use (something) to bad effect or for a bad purpose" or "to treat (a person or animal) with cruelty or violence, especially regularly or repeatedly."

Merriam-Webster defines abuse as "the improper usage or treatment of an entity, often to unfairly or improperly gain benefit."

Mentalhelp.net defines abuse as "when people mistreat or misuse other people, showing no concern for their integrity or innate worth as individuals, and in a manner that degrades their well-being. Abusers frequently are interested in controlling their victims. They . . . manipulate their victims into submission or compliance with their will."

How do you define abuse?_____

I can't see your definition of abuse, but if it's anything like the other three, it's probably safe to argue that nation-states both abuse and gaslight Indigenous people. But because of how ingrained extraction mentality is, the nation-state abuses and gaslights its non-Indigenous citizens, too. Consider this condensed history:

- Women were considered men's property for hundreds of years.
- Nearly all of the wealth of so-called first-world countries is a direct result of trafficking Black people in the transatlantic slave trade. Even after the thirteenth amendment abolished slavery in the U.S. in 1865, Black people were still denied full and equal rights because of Jim Crow laws, a system of segregation that remained in place for nearly a hundred years. In Canada, contrary to popular belief, slave ownership was actually widespread for over two hundred years. Black people living in Canada were not legally considered "people" until 1834.
- Japanese Canadians were forcibly interned during World War Two at their own expense, and their property and finances were seized and sold well below market value to pay for it. Unlike in the U.S., Canadian officials did not offer Japanese Canadians food or clothing during their internment. They had to buy everything themselves. There was no apology or financial redress from the federal government until 1988.
- After thousands of Chinese men built Canada's railroads, the Chinese head tax was imposed to keep the families of

these men out of Canada. In 1913, California passed the first alien land law, which prohibited "aliens ineligible for citizenship" from owning or leasing land. This law was only used against Asian immigrants, and was designed to give white farmers an unfair economic advantage over Asian farmers. Similar laws were rolled out across twelve other states. Alien land laws are still written into the state constitutions of both Florida and New Mexico.

- Labour laws to protect the working class — including rules on minimum wage, paid and unpaid breaks, and vacation time — exist only because unions organized and demanded them.

- There wasn't a United Nations Declaration on the Rights of Disabled Persons until 1975.

- Gay marriage wasn't legalized in Canada until 2005. And not fully in the United States until 2015.

- Trans people weren't legally protected from hate crimes in Canada until 2017. In the United States, there are no federal laws that ban discrimination against trans people or gay people in public accommodations, such as shops and restaurants. While states like Colorado,

Iowa, and Oregon and cities like San Francisco and New York City have laws which specifically grant trans people the right to access the public bathrooms that match their gender identity, other states and cities often have no clear protections. Cities like Chicago still allow businesses to restrict trans people from using public bathrooms that match their gender identity.

Even when these governments didn't see certain people as people, it still used them, extracting their labour and turning it into profit, then using their desire to be accepted by the nation state to coerce them into settling Indigenous lands and erasing Indigenous presence. And all the while Canada and the U.S. have told them that there's nothing wrong with the way they've been treated, or the way they've been encouraged to treat others; that if they've felt dehumanized, they're imagining it.

How often have you felt dehumanized this month?_____

This week?_____

Today?_____

318

Here are another few questions I don't expect you to answer: If the nations we live in are abusive, if they gaslight us, and if their profit margins and legitimacy as nations depend on abusing and gaslighting us, how can these nations ever really stop abuse and gaslighting? Why would they want to?

In that way, the U.S. and Canadian governments remind me of one of those estranged parents that hangs out on message boards. They hurt people they claim to value, hurt people they don't value, then when those people finally decide they want nothing to do with the abusers anymore, they ask what they did wrong, hapless, helpless.

Just like those estranged parents, our governments know very well what they did. What they continue to do.

My dad still sends me links to writing contests and articles he thinks I'll find interesting. He still tries to schmooze with people on my behalf, hoping to pry open the door to success just enough for me to slide through. He still jokes with me and lets me make jokes at his expense. His laugh still is the one sure way to make me laugh.

And he still does things that make me furious, that make me wonder if he can ever apologize for the past the way I need him to, or make things right the way I think he needs to make things right. He still does things that reaffirm my belief that he will almost always put his own interests first. He still does things that make me question why I continue to talk to him.

But a few years ago he started hugging me. He started saying he loved me before leaving or hanging up the phone. Neither of these were things he'd done often when I was growing up. I didn't realize how much I needed those hugs, those words, before I had them. And now that I do, I don't know if I want to let them go. I don't know if I can.

I want to hold my father accountable for the pain he's caused while still loving him for the joy he's created. I want to acknowledge him as a victim, honouring him for what he's had to survive, without enabling him or criminalizing him as an abuser. I want the nations and communities we live in to stop holding individuals to different standards than they hold themselves to — to dismantle abuse and gaslighting at all levels, micro and macro.

I want you to feel safe being vulnerable.

I want us both to be safe being vulnerable.

■ ■ ■ ■

What do you want?_____

Are those desires based on extraction?_____

Are they dependent upon capitalism or colonialism?_____

If the answers to those last two questions are yes, please revisit the first question.

ACKNOWLEDGEMENTS

Success is never achieved in isolation. There are so many people in my life I'm grateful for who have helped me achieve this dream.

Nya:wen to Ryan Harrington for your careful, insightful editing of this book. Your suggestions were always generous and respectful. I will always be thankful for your compassion and patience.

Nya:wen to the entire Melville House team for your enthusiasm and belief in this book.

Nya:wen to Marina Drukman for creating the breathtaking art that graces the cover of this book.

Nya:wen to my agents, Samantha Haywood and Stephanie Sinclair, for your unwavering support. You are all I could hope for.

Nya:wen to all of the editors I've worked with on the previously published essays in this collection. Your attention and talent made each piece worth republishing.

Nya:wen to some of my earliest teachers, Shyam Selvadurai and Michael Helm, for sharing your wisdom and getting me to read the best writing.

Nya:wen to my Creative Writing cohort at York University for being generous with their praise and constructive criticism.

Nya:wen to Roxane Gay, who probably doesn't remember publishing an early version of "Half-Breed" on *The Butter,* but whose acceptance came when I needed it most.

Nya:wen to Leanne Betasamosake Simpson, whose writing has shaped me and whose support has nourished me. If she hadn't asked me to submit to *The Malahat Review* issue she was editing, then reminded me to submit again close to the deadline, I would never have written the title essay in this collection, and she wouldn't have suggested the perfect title.

Nya:wen to Waubgeshig Rice and Cherie Dimaline, who both believed in me the moment I met them in Banff. They offered me mentorship and guidance, suggested places to submit my work and made the confusing world of grant-writing much more understandable.

Nya:wen to Jack Illingworth and the

wonderful people at the OAC. The grants I've received from your incredible organization have helped me create a writing life for myself.

Nya:wen to both my Banff crews for showing me the power of BIPOC community. Every one of you has talent that continues to excite, inspire and astonish me.

Nya:wen to Tanya Talaga for your incredible writing, brilliance, generosity and care. I'll never get over you choosing me for the RBC Taylor Emerging Writer Award. I hope I can live up to your faith in me.

Nya:wen to every Indigenous writer who came before me and all who will come after me. You have made and will continue to make Indigenous lit matter.

Nya:wen to Native Twitter for creating a space where I could find my voice and feel the warmth of community, especially when I couldn't be at Six Nations.

Nya:wen to the people of Six Nations of the Grand River territory for being strong, brilliant badasses. You've all taught me how to resist and how to reclaim.

Nya:wen to all the friends who have encouraged me and offered me the gift of their friendship throughout the writing of this book. Special thanks to Brandi Dunn, Gwen Benaway and Chelsea Rooney, who are some of the best friends I've ever had and who I love dearly.

Nya:wen to my beautiful family. Dad, Mom, Missy, Jon, Mikey, Dakota, Melita, Teena, Linnie, Gracie, Patty, all of my aunties, uncles and cousins. You all taught me how to laugh loud and love deep. Words can't express how much I appreciate each of you. I wouldn't have made it without you.

Nya:wen to Miles, who has taught me so much already even though you're only 12. Being your mother is the best thing I've ever done. I love you.

Nya:wen to Mike, my husband, editor, writing partner and best friend. You have made me a better person and writer in every way imaginable. I'll never be able to repay you for your brilliance, patience, humour, care, love and friendship, but I'll spend every day of my life trying.

Finally, nya:wen to you, reader, for offering me the gift of your time and attention. I hope my little book earned it.

ABOUT THE AUTHOR

Alicia Elliott is an award-winning Mohawk writer. Her writing has been published by *The Washington Post, The Toast, Vice, Maclean's* and many others. She is currently creative nonfiction editor at *The Fiddlehead.* She was the 2017–18 Geoffrey and Margaret Andrew Fellow at UBC, and received the RBC Taylor Emerging Writer Award in 2018. Her fiction has appeared in *Best American Short Stories 2018, The Journey Prize Stories 30* and *Best Canadian Stories 2018. A Mind Spread Out on the Ground,* her first book, was a bestseller in Canada, and was shortlisted for the Hilary Weston Prize for Nonfiction. Alicia lives in Brantford, Ontario, with her husband, child and Yorkie.

The employees of Thorndike Press hope you have enjoyed this Large Print book. All our Thorndike, Wheeler, and Kennebec Large Print titles are designed for easy reading, and all our books are made to last. Other Thorndike Press Large Print books are available at your library, through selected bookstores, or directly from us.

For information about titles, please call:
  (800) 223-1244

or visit our website at:
  gale.com/thorndike

To share your comments, please write:
  Publisher
  Thorndike Press
  10 Water St., Suite 310
  Waterville, ME 04901